C# 7 Quick Syntax Reference

A Pocket Guide to the Language, APIs, and Library

Second Edition

Mikael Olsson

Apress®

C# 7 Quick Syntax Reference: A Pocket Guide to the Language, APIs, and Library

Mikael Olsson
Hammarland, Länsi-Suomi, Finland

ISBN-13 (pbk): 978-1-4842-3816-5   ISBN-13 (electronic): 978-1-4842-3817-2
https://doi.org/10.1007/978-1-4842-3817-2

Library of Congress Control Number: 2018954673

Managing Director, Apress Media LLC: Welmoed Spahr
Acquisitions Editor: Steve Anglin
Development Editor: Matthew Moodie
Coordinating Editor: Mark Powers

Cover designed by eStudioCalamar

Cover image designed by Freepik (www.freepik.com)

Distributed to the book trade worldwide by Springer Science+Business Media New York, 233 Spring Street, 6th Floor, New York, NY 10013. Phone 1-800-SPRINGER, fax (201) 348-4505, e-mail orders-ny@springer-sbm.com, or visit www.springeronline.com. Apress Media, LLC is a California LLC and the sole member (owner) is Springer Science + Business Media Finance Inc (SSBM Finance Inc). SSBM Finance Inc is a **Delaware** corporation.

For information on translations, please e-mail editorial@apress.com; for reprint, paperback, or audio rights, please email bookpermissions@springernature.com.

Apress titles may be purchased in bulk for academic, corporate, or promotional use. eBook versions and licenses are also available for most titles. For more information, reference our Print and eBook Bulk Sales web page at http://www.apress.com/bulk-sales.

Any source code or other supplementary material referenced by the author in this book is available to readers on GitHub via the book's product page, located at www.apress.com/9781484238165. For more detailed information, please visit http://www.apress.com/source-code.

Printed on acid-free paper

Table of Contents

About the Author

Mikael Olsson is a professional web entrepreneur, programmer, and author. He works for an R&D company in Finland, where he specializes in software development. In his spare time he writes books and creates websites that summarize various fields of interest. The books he writes are focused on teaching their subjects in the most efficient way possible, by explaining only what is relevant and practical without any unnecessary repetition or theory. The portal to his online businesses and other websites is Siforia.com.

About the Technical Reviewer

 **Michael Thomas** has worked in software development for more than 20 years as an individual contributor, team lead, program manager, and vice president of engineering. Michael has more than 10 years of experience working with mobile devices. His current focus is in the medical sector, using mobile devices to accelerate information transfer between patients and health care providers.

Introduction

The C# programming language is an object-oriented language created by Microsoft for the .NET Framework. C# (pronounced "see sharp") builds on some of the best features of the major programming languages. It combines the power of C++ with the simplicity of Visual Basic and also borrows much from Java. This results in a language that is easy to learn and use, robust against errors, and enables rapid application development. All this is achieved without sacrificing much of the power or speed, when compared to C++.

In the years following its release in 2002, C# has grown to become one of the most popular programming languages. It is a general-purpose programming language, so it is useful for creating a wide range of programs. Everything from small utilities to computer games, desktop applications, or even operating systems can be built in C#. The language can also be used with ASP.NET to create web-based applications.

When developing in .NET, programmers are given a wide range of choices as to which programming language to use. Some of the more popular .NET languages include VB.NET, C++/CLI, F#, and C#. Among these, C# is often the language of choice. Like the other .NET languages, C# is initially compiled to an intermediate language. This language is called the Common Intermediate Language (CIL) and is run on the .NET Framework. A .NET program will therefore be able to execute on any system that has this framework installed.

The .NET Framework is a software framework that includes a common execution engine and a rich class library. It runs on Microsoft Windows and is therefore only used for writing Windows applications. However, there are also cross-platform ports available, the two largest being Mono[1] and .NET Core.[2] These are both open source projects that allow .NET applications to be run on other platforms, such as Linux, MacOS, and embedded systems.

---

[1]http://www.mono-project.com
[2]https://docs.microsoft.com/dotnet/core

CHAPTER 1

Hello World

Choosing an IDE

To begin coding in C#, you need an Integrated Development Environment (IDE) that supports the Microsoft .NET Framework. The most popular choice is Microsoft's own Visual Studio.[1] This IDE is available for free as a light version called Visual Studio Community, which can be downloaded from the Visual Studio website.[2]

The C# language has undergone a number of updates since the initial release of C# 1.0 in 2002. At the time of writing, C# 7.3 is the current version and was released in 2018. Each version of the language corresponds to a version of Visual Studio, so in order to use the features of C# 7.3 you need Visual Studio 2017 (version 15.7 or higher).

Creating a Project

After installing the IDE, go ahead and launch it. You then need to create a new project, which will manage the C# source files and other resources. To display the New Project window, go to File ➤ New ➤ Project in Visual Studio. From there select the Visual C# template type in the left frame. Then select the Console App template in the right frame. At the bottom of

---

[1]http://www.visualstudio.com
[2]https://www.visualstudio.com/vs/community/

© Mikael Olsson 2018
M. Olsson, *C# 7 Quick Syntax Reference*, https://doi.org/10.1007/978-1-4842-3817-2_1

1

the window you can configure the name and location of the project if you want to. When you are done, click OK and the project wizard will create your project.

You have now created a C# project. In the Solution Explorer pane (View ➤ Solution Explorer), you can see that the project consists of a single C# source file (.cs) that should already be opened. If not, you can double-click on the file in the Solution Explorer in order to open it. In the source file there is some basic code to help you get started. However, to keep things simple at this stage, go ahead and simplify the code into this.

```
class MyApp
{
  static void Main()
  {
  }
}
```

The application now consists of a class called MyApp containing an empty Main method, both delimited by curly brackets. The Main method is the entry point of the program and must have this format. The casing is also important since C# is case-sensitive. The curly brackets delimit what belongs to a code entity, such as a class or method, and they must be included. The brackets, along with their content, are referred to as code blocks, or just blocks.

Hello World

As is common when learning a new programming language, the first program to write is one that displays a "Hello World" text string. This is accomplished by adding the following line of code between the curly brackets of the Main method.

```
System.Console.WriteLine("Hello World");
```

This line of code uses the WriteLine method, which accepts a single string parameter delimited by double quotes. The method is located inside the Console class, which belongs to the System namespace. Note that the dot operator (.) is used to access members of both namespaces and classes. The statement must end with a semicolon, as must all statements in C#. Your code should now look like this.

```
class MyApp
{
  static void Main()
  {
    System.Console.WriteLine("Hello World");
  }
}
```

The WriteLine method adds a line break at the end of the printed string. To display a string without a line break, you use the Write method instead.

IntelliSense

When writing code in Visual Studio a window called IntelliSense will pop up wherever there are multiple predetermined alternatives from which to choose. This window is very useful and can be brought up manually by pressing Ctrl+Space. It gives you quick access to any code entities you are able to use within your program, including the classes and methods of the .NET Framework along with their descriptions. This is a very powerful feature that you should learn to use.

CHAPTER 2

Compile and Run

Visual Studio Compilation

With the Hello World program completed, the next step is to compile and run it. To do so, open the Debug menu and select Start Without Debugging, or simply press Ctrl+F5. Visual Studio will then compile and run the application, which displays the string in a console window.

The reason why you do not want to choose the Start Debugging command (F5) here is because the console window will then close as soon as the program has finished executing.

Console Compilation

If you did not have an IDE such as Visual Studio, you could still compile the program as long as you have the .NET Framework installed. To try this, open a console window (`C:\Windows\System32\cmd.exe`) and navigate to the project folder where the source file is located. You then need to find the C# compiler called `csc.exe`, which is located in a path similar to the one shown here. Run the compiler with the source filename as an argument and it will produce an executable in the current folder.

```
C:\MySolution\MyProject>
\Windows\Microsoft.NET\Framework64\v2.0.50727\
csc.exe Program.cs
```

© Mikael Olsson 2018
M. Olsson, *C# 7 Quick Syntax Reference*, https://doi.org/10.1007/978-1-4842-3817-2_2

If you try running the compiled program it will show the same output as the one created by Visual Studio.

```
C:\MySolution\MyProject> Program.exe
Hello World
```

Language Version

A project in Visual Studio will by default compile using the latest major version of the language, which is currently C# 7.0. To use the latest features from minor language updates (C# 7.1, 7.2, and 7.3), you need to update the settings for your project. To do so first right-click the project node in the Solution Explorer and select Properties. From there, click on the Build tab on the left and then the Advanced button in the bottom right. A new window appears where you can change the language version from a drop-down list. Change the selection to C# Latest Minor Version (Latest). Click OK and then close the Properties tab and you will have enabled the most recent features of C#.

Comments

Comments are used to insert notes into the source code. C# uses the standard C++ comment notations, with both single-line and multi-line comments. They are meant only to enhance the readability of the source code and have no effect on the end program. The single-line comment begins with // and extends to the end of the line. The multi-line comment may span multiple lines and is delimited by /* and */.

```
// single-line comment

/* multi-line
   comment */
```

In addition to these, there are two documentation comments. There is one single-line documentation comment that starts with ///, and one multi-line documentation comment that is delimited by /** and */. These comments are used when producing class documentation.

```
/// <summary>Class level documentation.</summary>
class MyApp
{
  /** <summary>Program entry point.</summary>
      <param name="args">Command line arguments.</param>
   */
  static void Main(string[] args)
  {
    System.Console.WriteLine("Hello World");
  }
}
```

CHAPTER 3

Variables

Variables are used for storing data in memory during program execution.

Data Types

Depending on what data you need to store, there are several different kinds of data types. The *simple types* in C# consist of four signed integer types and four unsigned, three floating-point types, as well as char and bool.

Data Type	Size (Bits)	Description
sbyte	8	Signed integers
short	16	
int	32	
long	64	
byte	8	Unsigned integers
ushort	16	
uint	32	
ulong	64	
float	32	Floating-point numbers
double	64	
decimal	128	
char	16	Unicode character
bool	4	Boolean value

© Mikael Olsson 2018
M. Olsson, *C# 7 Quick Syntax Reference*, https://doi.org/10.1007/978-1-4842-3817-2_3

Declaration

In C#, a variable must be *declared* (created) before it can be used. To declare a variable, you start with the data type you want it to hold followed by a variable name. The name can be almost anything you want, but it is a good idea to give your variables names that are closely related to the value they will hold.

```
int myInt;
```

Assignment

A value is assigned to the variable by using the equals sign, which is the assignment operator (=). The variable then becomes *defined* or *initialized*.

```
myInt = 10;
```

The declaration and assignment can be combined into a single statement.

```
int myInt = 10;
```

If multiple variables of the same type are needed, there is a shorthand way of declaring or defining them by using the comma operator (,).

```
int myInt = 10, myInt2 = 20, myInt3;
```

Once a variable has been defined (declared and assigned), it can be used by referencing the variable's name.

```
System.Console.Write(myInt); // "10"
```

Integer Types

There are four signed integer types that can be used depending on how large a number you need the variable to hold.

```
// Signed integers
sbyte myInt8  = 2; // -128   to +127
short myInt16 = 1; // -32768 to +32767
int   myInt32 = 0; // -2^31  to +2^31-1
long  myInt64 =-1; // -2^63  to +2^63-1
```

The unsigned types can be used if you only need to store positive values.

```
// Unsigned integers
byte   uInt8  = 0;  // 0 to 255
ushort uInt16 = 1;  // 0 to 65535
uint   uInt32 = 2;  // 0 to 2^32-1
ulong  uInt64 = 3;  // 0 to 2^64-1
```

In addition to the standard decimal notation, integers can also be assigned using hexadecimal notation. As of C# 7.0, there is a binary notation as well. Hexadecimal numbers are prefixed with 0x and binary numbers with 0b.

```
int myHex = 0xF;    // 15 in hexadecimal (base 16)
int myBin = 0b0100; // 4 in binary (base 2)
```

Version 7.0 of C# also added a digit separator (_) to improve readability of long numbers. This digit separator can appear anywhere within the number, as well as at the beginning of the number as of C# 7.2.

```
int myBin = 0b_0010_0010; // 34 in binary notation (0b)
```

Floating-Point Types

The floating-point types can store real numbers with different levels of precision. Constant floating-point numbers in C# are always kept as doubles, so in order to assign such a number to a float variable, an F character needs to be appended to convert the number to the float type. The same applies to the M character for decimals.

```
float   myFloat   = 3.14F; // 7 digits of precision
double  myDouble  = 3.14;  // 15-16 digits of precision
decimal myDecimal = 3.14M; // 28-29 digits of precision
```

A more common and useful way to convert between data types is to use an explicit cast. An *explicit cast* is performed by placing the desired data type in parentheses before the variable or constant that is to be converted. This will convert the value to the specified type, in this case float, before the assignment occurs.

```
myFloat = (float) myDecimal; // explicit cast
```

The precisions shown earlier refer to the total number of digits that the types can hold. For example, when attempting to assign more than seven digits to a float, the least significant ones will get rounded off.

```
myFloat = 12345.6789F; // rounded to 12345.68
```

Floating-point numbers can be assigned using either decimal or exponential notation, as in the following example.

```
myDouble = 3e2; // 3*10^2 = 300
```

Char Type

The char type can contain a single Unicode character delimited by single quotes.

```
char c = '3'; // Unicode char
```

Bool Type

The bool type can store a Boolean value, which is a value that can be either true or false. These values are specified with the true and false keywords.

```
bool b = true; // bool value
```

Variable Scope

The *scope* of a variable refers to the code block within which it is possible to use that variable without qualification. For example, a local variable is a variable declared within a method. Such a variable will only be available within that method's code block, after it has been declared. Once the scope of the method ends, the local variable will be destroyed.

```
static void Main()
{
  int localVar; // local variable
}
```

In addition to local variables, C# has field and parameter type variables, which will be looked at in later chapters. However, C# does not have global variables, unlike C++.

CHAPTER 4

Operators

Operators are special symbols used to operate on values. They can be grouped into five types: arithmetic, assignment, comparison, logical, and bitwise operators.

Arithmetic Operators

The arithmetic operators include the four basic arithmetic operations, as well as the modulus operator (%), which is used to obtain the division remainder.

```
float x = 3 + 2; // 5 // addition
      x = 3 - 2; // 1 // subtraction
      x = 3 * 2; // 6 // multiplication
      x = 3 / 2; // 1 // division
      x = 3 % 2; // 1 // modulus (division remainder)
```

Notice that the division sign gives an incorrect result. This is because it operates on two integer values and will therefore round the result and return an integer. To get the correct value, one of the numbers needs to be converted into a floating-point number.

```
x = 3 / (float)2; // 1.5
```

© Mikael Olsson 2018
M. Olsson, *C# 7 Quick Syntax Reference*, https://doi.org/10.1007/978-1-4842-3817-2_4

Assignment Operators

The next group is the assignment operators. Most importantly is the assignment operator (=) itself, which assigns a value to a variable.

Combined Assignment Operators

A common use of the assignment and arithmetic operators is to operate on a variable and then to save the result back into that same variable. These operations can be shortened with the combined assignment operators.

```
int x = 0;
    x += 5; // x = x+5;
    x -= 5; // x = x-5;
    x *= 5; // x = x*5;
    x /= 5; // x = x/5;
    x %= 5; // x = x%5;
```

Increment and Decrement Operators

Another common operation is to increment or decrement a variable by one. This can be simplified with the increment (++) and decrement (--) operators.

```
x++; // x = x+1;
x--; // x = x-1;
```

Both of these operators can be used before or after a variable.

```
x++; // post-increment
x--; // post-decrement
++x; // pre-increment
--x; // pre-decrement
```

The result on the variable is the same whichever is used. The difference is that the post-operator returns the original value before it changes the variable, while the pre-operator changes the variable first and then returns the value.

```
int x, y;
x = 5; y = x++; // y=5, x=6
x = 5; y = ++x; // y=6, x=6
```

Comparison Operators

The comparison operators compare two values and return true or false. They are mainly used to specify conditions, which are expressions that evaluate to true or false.

```
bool b = (2 == 3); // equal to (false)
     b = (2 != 3); // not equal to (true)
     b = (2 > 3);  // greater than (false)
     b = (2 < 3);  // less than (true)
     b = (2 >= 3); // greater than or equal to (false)
     b = (2 <= 3); // less than or equal to (true)
```

Logical Operators

The logical operators are often used together with the comparison operators. Logical and (&&) evaluates to true if both the left and right side are true, and logical or (||) evaluates to true if either the left or right side is true. The logical not (!) operator is used for inverting a Boolean result. Note that for both "logical and" and "logical or," the right side of the operator will not be evaluated if the result is already determined by the left side.

```
bool b = (true && false); // logical and (false)
     b = (true || false); // logical or (true)
     b = !(true);         // logical not (false)
```

Bitwise Operators

The bitwise operators can manipulate individual bits inside an integer. For example, the bitwise and (&) operator makes the resulting bit 1 if the corresponding bits on both sides of the operator are set.

```
int x = 5 & 4;  // and (0b101 & 0b100 = 0b100 = 4)
    x = 5 | 4;  // or (0b101 | 0b100 = 0b101 = 5)
    x = 5 ^ 4;  // xor (0b101 ^ 0b100 = 0b001 = 1)
    x = 4 << 1; // left shift (0b100 << 1 = 0b1000 = 8)
    x = 4 >> 1; // right shift (0b100 >> 1 = 0b10 = 2)
    x = ~4;     // invert (~0b00000100 = 0b11111011 = -5)
```

These bitwise operators have shorthand assignment operators, just like the arithmetic operators.

```
int x=5; x &= 4;  // and (0b101 & 0b100 = 0b100 = 4)
    x=5; x |= 4;  // or (0b101 | 0b100 = 0b101 = 5)
    x=5; x ^= 4;  // xor (0b101 ^ 0b100 = 0b001 = 1)
    x=5; x <<= 1; // left shift (0b101 << 1 = 0b1010 = 10)
    x=5; x >>= 1; // right shift (0b101 >> 1 = 0b10 = 2)
```

Operator Precedents

In C#, expressions are normally evaluated from left to right. However, when an expression contains multiple operators, the precedence of those operators decides the order in which they are evaluated. The order of precedence can be seen in the following table, where the operator with the greater precedence will be evaluated first.

Pre	Operator	Pre	Operator
1	++ -- ! ~	7	&
2	* / %	8	^
3	+ -	9	|
4	<< >>	10	&&
5	< <= > >=	11	||
6	== !=	12	= op=

For example, logical and (&&) binds weaker than relational operators, which in turn bind weaker than arithmetic operators.

```
bool x = 2+3 > 1*4 && 5/5 == 1; // true
```

To make things clearer, parentheses can be used to specify which part of the expression will be evaluated first. Parentheses have the greatest precedence of all operators.

```
bool x = ((2+3) > (1*4)) && ((5/5) == 1); // true
```

CHAPTER 5

Strings

The *string* data type is used to store string constants. They are delimited by double quotes.

```
string a = "Hello";
```

String Concatenation

The concatenation operator (+) can combine strings together. It also has an accompanying assignment operator (+=), which appends a string to another and creates a new string.

```
string b = a + " World"; // Hello World
a += " World";           // Hello World
```

When one of the operands is not of a string type, the concatenation operator will implicitly convert the non-string type into a string, making the following assignment valid.

```
int i = 1;
string c = i + " is " + 1; // 1 is 1
```

The string conversion is performed implicitly using the ToString method. All types in .NET have this method, which provides a string representation of a variable or expression. As seen in the next example, the string conversion can also be made explicitly.

```
string d = i.ToString() + " is " + 1.ToString(); // 1 is 1
```

© Mikael Olsson 2018
M. Olsson, *C# 7 Quick Syntax Reference*, https://doi.org/10.1007/978-1-4842-3817-2_5

Another way to compile strings is to use string interpolation. This feature was added in C# 6 and enables expressions placed inside curly brackets to be evaluated within a string. To perform string interpolation, a dollar sign ($) is placed before the string.

```
string s1 = "Hello";
string s2 = "World";
string s = $"{s1} {s2}"; // Hello World
```

Escape Characters

A statement can be broken up across multiple lines, but a string constant must be on a single line. In order to divide it, the string constant has to first be split up using the concatenation operator.

```
string myString
        = "Hello " +
          "World";
```

To add new lines into the string itself, the escape character (\n) is used.

```
string myString = "Hello\nWorld";
```

This backslash notation is used to write special characters, such as a backslash itself or a double quote. Among the special characters is also a Unicode character notation for writing any character.

Character	Meaning	Character	Meaning
\n	Newline	\f	Form feed
\t	Horizontal tab	\a	Alert sound
\v	Vertical tab	\'	Single quote
\b	Backspace	\"	Double quote
\r	Carriage return	\\	Backslash
\0	Null character	\uFFFF	Unicode character (four-digit hex number)

Escape characters can be ignored by adding an @ symbol before the string. This is called a *verbatim string* and can be used to make file paths more readable, for example.

```
string s1 = "c:\\Windows\\System32\\cmd.exe";
string s2 = @"c:\Windows\System32\cmd.exe";
```

String Compare

The way to compare two strings is simply by using the equal to operator (==). This will not compare the memory addresses, as in some other languages such as Java.

```
string greeting = "Hi";
bool b = (greeting == "Hi"); // true
```

String Members

The string type is an alias for the String class. As such, it provides a multitude of methods related to strings. For example, methods like Replace, Insert, and Remove. An important thing to note is that there are no methods for changing a string. Methods that appear to modify a string actually always return a completely new string. This is because the String class is immutable. The content of a string variable cannot be changed unless the whole string is replaced.

```
string a = "String";
string b = a.Replace("i", "o"); // Strong
       b = a.Insert(0, "My ");  // My String
       b = a.Remove(0, 3);      // ing
       b = a.Substring(0, 3);   // Str
       b = a.ToUpper();         // STRING
int    i = a.Length;            // 6
```

23

StringBuilder Class

StringBuilder is a mutable string class. Because of the performance cost associated with replacing a string, the StringBuilder class is a better alternative when a string needs to be modified many times.

```
System.Text.StringBuilder sb = new
System.Text.StringBuilder("Hello");
```

The class has several methods that can be used to manipulate the actual content of a string, such as Append, Remove, and Insert.

```
sb.Append(" World");    // Hello World
sb.Remove(0, 5);        // World
sb.Insert(0, "Bye");    // Bye World
```

To convert a StringBuilder object back into a regular string, you use the ToString method.

```
string s = sb.ToString(); // Bye World
```

CHAPTER 6

Arrays

An *array* is a data structure used for storing a collection of values that all have the same data type.

Array Declaration

To declare an array, a set of square brackets is appended to the data type that the array will contain, followed by the array's name. An array can be declared with any data type and all of its elements will then be of that type.

```
int[] x; // integer array
```

Array Allocation

The array is allocated with the new keyword, followed again by the data type and a set of square brackets containing the length of the array. This is the fixed number of elements that the array can contain. Once the array is created, the elements will automatically be assigned to the default value for that data type, in this case zero.

```
int[] x = new int[3];
```

© Mikael Olsson 2018
M. Olsson, *C# 7 Quick Syntax Reference*, https://doi.org/10.1007/978-1-4842-3817-2_6

Array Assignment

To fill the array elements, they can be referenced one at a time and then assigned values. An array element is referenced by placing the element's index inside square brackets. Notice that the index for the first element starts with zero.

```
x[0] = 1;
x[1] = 2;
x[2] = 3;
```

Alternatively, the values can be assigned all at once by using a curly bracket notation. The new keyword and data type may optionally be left out if the array is declared at the same time.

```
int[] y = new int[] { 1, 2, 3 };
int[] z = { 1, 2, 3 };
```

Array Access

Once the array elements are initialized, they can be accessed by referencing the elements' indexes inside the square brackets.

```
System.Console.Write(x[0] + x[1] + x[2]); // "6"
```

Rectangular Arrays

There are two kinds of multi-dimensional arrays in C#: rectangular and jagged. A rectangular array has the same length of all sub-arrays and separates the dimensions using a comma.

```
string[,] x = new string[2, 2];
```

As with single-dimensional arrays, they can either be filled in one at a time or all at once during the allocation.

```
x[0, 0] = "00"; x[0, 1] = "01";
x[1, 0] = "10"; x[1, 1] = "11";
string[,] y = { { "00", "01" }, { "10", "11" } };
```

Jagged Arrays

Jagged arrays are arrays of arrays, and they can have irregular dimensions. The dimensions are allocated one at a time and the sub-arrays can therefore be allocated to different sizes.

```
string[][] a = new string[2][];
a[0] = new string[1]; a[0][0] = "00";
a[1] = new string[2]; a[1][0] = "10"; a[1][1] = "11";
```

It is possible to assign the values during the allocation.

```
string[][] b = { new string[] { "00" },
                 new string[] { "10", "11" } };
```

These are all examples of two-dimensional arrays. If you need more than two dimensions, more commas can be added for the rectangular array, or more square brackets for the jagged array.

CHAPTER 7

Conditionals

Conditional statements are used to execute different code blocks based on different conditions.

If Statement

The if statement will execute only if the condition inside the parentheses is evaluated to true. The condition can include any of the comparison and logical operators.

```
int x = new System.Random().Next(3); // gives 0, 1 or 2
if (x < 1) {
  System.Console.Write(x + " < 1");
}
```

To test for other conditions, the if statement can be extended by any number of else if clauses. Each additional condition will be tested only if all previous conditions are false.

```
else if (x > 1) {
  System.Console.Write(x + " > 1");
}
```

The if statement can have one else clause at the end, which will execute if all previous conditions are false.

© Mikael Olsson 2018
M. Olsson, *C# 7 Quick Syntax Reference*, https://doi.org/10.1007/978-1-4842-3817-2_7

```
else {
  System.Console.Write(x + " == 1");
}
```

As for the curly brackets, they can be left out if only a single statement needs to be executed conditionally. However, it is considered good practice to include them since they improve readability.

```
if (x < 1)
  System.Console.Write(x + " < 1");
else if (x > 1)
  System.Console.Write(x + " > 1");
else
  System.Console.Write(x + " == 1");
```

Switch Statement

The switch statement checks for equality between either an integer or a string and a series of case labels, and then passes execution to the matching case. The statement can contain any number of case clauses and may end with a default label for handling all other cases.

```
int x = new System.Random().Next(3); // gives 0, 1 or 2
switch (x)
{
  case 0: System.Console.Write(x + " is 0"); break;
  case 1: System.Console.Write(x + " is 1"); break;
  default:System.Console.Write(x + " is 2"); break;
}
```

Note that the statements after each case label are not surrounded by curly brackets. Instead, the statements end with the break keyword to break out of the switch. Unlike many other languages, case clauses in C#

must end with a jump statement, such as break. This means that the break keyword cannot be left out to allow the execution to fall through to the next label. The reason for this is that an unintentional fall-through is a common programming error.

Goto Statement

To cause a fall-through to occur, this behavior has to be explicitly specified using the goto jump statement followed by a case label. This will cause the execution to jump to that label.

```
case 0: goto case 1;
```

Goto may be used outside of switches to jump to a label in the same method's scope. Control may then be transferred out of a nested scope, but not into a nested scope. However, using goto in this manner is discouraged since it makes it difficult to follow the flow of execution.

```
goto myLabel;
// ...
myLabel:
```

Ternary Operator

In addition to the if and switch statements, there is the ternary operator (?:). This operator can replace a single if-else clause that assigns a value to a specific variable. The operator takes three expressions. If the first one is evaluated to true, then the second expression is returned, and if it is false, the third one is returned.

```
// Get a number between 0.0 and 1.0
double x = new System.Random().NextDouble();
x = (x < 0.5) ? 0 : 1; // ternary operator (?:)
```

31

CHAPTER 8

Loops

There are four looping structures in C#. These are used to execute a code block multiple times. Just as with the conditional if statement, the curly brackets for the loops can be left out if there is only one statement in the code block.

While Loop

The while loop runs through the code block only if its condition is true and will continue looping for as long as the condition remains true. Note that the condition is only checked at the beginning of each iteration (loop).

```
int i = 0;
while (i < 10) {
  System.Console.Write(i++); // 0-9
}
```

Do-while Loop

The do-while loop works in the same way as the while loop, except that it checks the condition after the code block and will therefore always run through the code block at least once. Bear in mind that this loop ends with a semicolon.

© Mikael Olsson 2018
M. Olsson, *C# 7 Quick Syntax Reference*, https://doi.org/10.1007/978-1-4842-3817-2_8

```
int j = 0;
do {
  System.Console.Write(j++); // 0-9
} while (j < 10);
```

For Loop

The for loop is used to go through a code block a specified number of times. It uses three parameters. The first parameter initializes a counter and is always executed once, before the loop. The second parameter holds the condition for the loop and is checked before each iteration. The third parameter contains the increment of the counter and is executed at the end of each iteration.

```
for (int k = 0; k < 10; k++) {
  System.Console.Write(k); // 0-9
}
```

The for loop has several possible variations. For instance, the first and third parameters can be split into several statements using the comma operator.

```
for (int k = 0, m = 5; k < 10; k++, m--) {
  System.Console.Write(k+m); // 5 (10x)
}
```

There is also the option of leaving out one or more of the parameters. For example, the third parameter may be moved into the body of the loop.

```
for (int k = 0; k < 10;) {
  System.Console.Write(k++); // 0-9
}
```

Foreach Loop

The foreach loop provides an easy way to iterate through arrays. At each iteration, the next element in the array is assigned to the specified variable (the iterator) and the loop continues to execute until it has gone through the entire array.

```
int[] a = { 1, 2, 3 };
foreach (int n in a) {
  System.Console.Write(n); // "123"
}
```

Note that the iterator variable is read-only and can therefore not be used to change elements in the array.

Break and Continue

There are two special keywords that can be used inside loops—break and continue. The break keyword ends the loop structure, and continue skips the rest of the current iteration and continues at the start of the next iteration.

```
for (int i = 0; i < 10; i++) {
  if (i == 5) break; // end loop
  if (i == 3) continue; // start next iteration
  System.Console.Write(i); // "0124"
}
```

CHAPTER 9

Methods

Methods are reusable code blocks that will only execute when called.

Defining Methods

A method can be created inside a class by typing void followed by the method's name, a set of parentheses, and a code block. The void keyword means that the method will not return a value. The naming convention for methods is the same as for classes—a descriptive name with each word initially capitalized.

```
class MyApp
{
  void MyPrint()
  {
    System.Console.WriteLine("Hello World");
  }
}
```

All methods in C# must belong to a class, and they are the only place where statements may be executed. C# does not have global functions, which are methods defined outside of classes.

Calling Methods

The previously defined method will print out a text message. To invoke (call) it, an instance of the MyApp class must first be created by using the new keyword. The dot operator is then used after the instance's name to access its members, which includes the MyPrint method.

```
class MyApp
{
  static void Main()
  {
    MyApp m = new MyApp();
    m.MyPrint(); // Hello World
  }

  void MyPrint()
  {
    System.Console.WriteLine("Hello World");
  }
}
```

Method Parameters

The parentheses that follow the method name are used to pass arguments to the method. To do this the corresponding parameters must first be specified in the method definition in the form of a comma-separated list of declarations.

```
void MyPrint(string s1, string s2)
{
  System.Console.WriteLine(s1 + s2);
}
```

A method can be defined to take any number of arguments, and they can have any data types. Just ensure the method is called with the same types and number of arguments.

```
static void Main()
{
  MyApp m = new MyApp();
  m.MyPrint("Hello", " World"); // "Hello World"
}
```

To be precise, *parameters* appear in method definitions, while *arguments* appear in method calls. However, the two terms are sometimes used interchangeably.

Params Keyword

To take a variable number of arguments of a specific type, an array with the params modifier can be added as the last parameter in the list. Any extra parameters of the specified type that are passed to the method will automatically be stored in that array.

```
void MyPrint(params string[] s)
{
  foreach (string x in s)
    System.Console.WriteLine(x);
}
```

Method Overloading

It is possible to declare multiple methods with the same name as long as the parameters vary in type or number. This is called *method overloading* and can be seen in the implementation of the System.Console.Write method, for example, which has 18 method definitions. It is a powerful feature that allows a method to handle a variety of arguments without the programmer needing to be aware of using different methods.

```
void MyPrint(string s)
{
  System.Console.WriteLine(s);
}

void MyPrint(int i)
{
  System.Console.WriteLine(i);
}
```

Optional Parameters

As of C# 4.0, parameters can be declared as optional by providing a default value for them in the method declaration. When the method is invoked, these optional arguments may be omitted to use the default values.

```
class MyApp
{
  void MySum(int i, int j = 0, int k = 0)
  {
    System.Console.WriteLine(1*i + 2*j + 3*k);
  }

  static void Main()
  {
    new MyApp().MySum(1, 2); // 5
  }
}
```

Named Arguments

C# 4.0 also introduced *named arguments,* which allow an argument to be passed using the name of its corresponding parameter. This feature complements optional parameters by enabling arguments to be passed out of order, instead of relying on their position in the parameter list. Therefore, any optional parameter can be specified without having to specify the value for every optional parameter before it.

```
static void Main()
{
  new MyApp().MySum(1, k: 2); // 7
}
```

Both optional and required parameters can be named, but the named arguments must be placed after the unnamed ones. This order restriction was loosened in C# 7.2, allowing named arguments to be followed by positional arguments provided that the named arguments are in the correct position.

```
static void Main()
{
  new MyApp().MySum(i: 2, 1); // 4
}
```

Named arguments are useful for improving code readability, by identifying what each argument represents.

Return Statement

A method can return a value. The void keyword is then replaced with the data type that the method will return, and the return keyword is added to the method body with an argument of the specified return type.

```
string GetPrint()
{
  return "Hello";
}
```

Return is a jump statement that causes the method to exit and return the value to the place where the method was called. For example, the GetPrint method can be passed as an argument to the WriteLine method since the method evaluates to a string.

```
static void Main()
{
  MyApp m = new MyApp();
  System.Console.WriteLine(m.GetPrint()); // "Hello World"
}
```

The return statement may also be used in void methods to exit before the end block is reached.

```
void MyMethod()
{
  return;
}
```

Value and Reference Types

There are two kinds of data types in C#: *value types* and *reference types*. Variables of value types directly contain their data, whereas variables of reference types hold references to their data. The reference types in C# include class, interface, array, and delegate types. The value types include the simple types, as well as the struct, enum, and nullable types. Reference type variables are typically created using the new keyword, although that is not always necessary, as for example in the case of string objects.

A variable of a reference type is generally called an *object*, although strictly speaking the object is the data that the variable refers to. With reference types, multiple variables can reference the same object, and therefore operations performed through one variable will affect any other variables that reference the same object. In contrast, with value types, each variable will store its own value and operations on one will not affect another.

Pass by Value

When passing parameters of value type, only a local copy of the variable is passed. This means that if the copy is changed, it will not affect the original variable.

```
void Set(int i) { i = 10; }

static void Main()
{
  MyApp m = new MyApp();
  int x = 0;              // value type
  m.Set(x);               // pass value of x
  System.Console.Write(x); // 0
}
```

Pass by Reference

For reference data types, C# uses true pass by reference. This means that when a reference type is passed, it is not only possible to change its state, but also to replace the entire object and have the change propagate back to the original object.

```
void Set(int[] i) { i = new int[] { 10 }; }

static void Main()
{
  MyApp m = new MyApp();
  int[] y = { 0 };              // reference type
  m.Set(y);                     // pass object reference
  System.Console.Write(y[0]); // 10
}
```

Ref Keyword

A variable of value type can be passed by reference by using the ref keyword, both in the caller and method declarations. This will cause the variable to be passed in by reference, and therefore changing it will update the original value.

```
void Set(ref int i) { i = 10; }

static void Main()
{
  MyApp m = new MyApp();
  int x = 0;                // value type
  m.Set(ref x);             // pass reference to value type
  System.Console.Write(x); // 10
}
```

Value types can be returned by reference starting with C# 7.0. The ref keyword is then added both before the return type and the return value. Bear in mind that the returned variable must have a lifetime that extends beyond the method's scope, so it cannot be a variable local to the method.

```
class MyClass
{
  public int myField = 5;
  public ref int GetField()
  {
    return ref myField;
  }
}
```

The caller can decide whether to retrieve the returned variable by value (as a copy) or by reference (as an alias). Note that when retrieving by reference, the ref keyword is used both before the method call and before the variable declaration.

```
class MyApp
{
  static void Main()
  {
    MyClass m = new MyClass();
    ref int myAlias = ref m.GetField(); // reference
    int myCopy = m.GetField(); // value copy

    myAlias = 10;
    System.Console.WriteLine(m.myField); // "10"
  }
}
```

Out Keyword

Sometimes you may want to pass an unassigned variable by reference and have it assigned in the method. However, using an unassigned local variable will give a compile-time error. For this situation, the out keyword can be used. It has the same function as ref, except that the compiler will allow use of the unassigned variable, and it will make sure the variable is assigned in the method.

```
void Set(out int i) { i = 10; }

static void Main()
{
  MyApp m = new MyApp();
  int x;                       // value type
  m.Set(out x);                // pass reference to unset value type
  System.Console.Write(x); // 10
}
```

With C# 7.0, it became possible to declare out variables in the argument list of a method call. This feature allows the previous example to be simplified in the following manner.

```
static void Main()
{
  MyApp m = new MyApp();
  m.Set(out int x);
  System.Console.Write(x); // 10
}
```

Local Methods

Starting with C# 7.0, a method can be defined inside another method. This is useful for limiting the scope of a method, in cases when the method is only called by one other method. To illustrate, a nested method is used here to perform a countdown. Note that this nested method calls itself and is therefore called a *recursive method*.

```
class MyClass
{
  void CountDown()
  {
    int x = 10;
    Recursion(x);
    System.Console.WriteLine("Done");

    void Recursion(int i)
    {
      if (i <= 0) return;
      System.Console.WriteLine(i);
      System.Threading.Thread.Sleep(1000); // wait 1 second
      Recursion(i - 1);
    }
  }

  static void Main()
  {
    new MyClass().CountDown();
  }
}
```

CHAPTER 10

Class

A *class* is a template used to create objects. They are made up of members, the main two of which are fields and methods. *Fields* are variables that hold the state of the object, while *methods* define what the object can do.

```csharp
class MyRectangle
{
  int x, y;
  int GetArea() { return x * y; }
}
```

Object Creation

To use a class's instance members from outside the defining class, an object of the class must first be created. This is done by using the new keyword, which will create a new object in the system's memory.

```csharp
class MyClass
{
  static void Main()
  {
    // Create an object of MyRectangle
    MyRectangle r = new MyRectangle();
  }
}
```

© Mikael Olsson 2018
M. Olsson, *C# 7 Quick Syntax Reference*, https://doi.org/10.1007/978-1-4842-3817-2_10

An object is also called an *instance*. The object will contain its own set of fields, which hold values that are different from those of other instances of the class.

Accessing Object Members

In addition to creating the object, the members of the class that are to be accessible need to be declared as public in the class definition.

```
class MyRectangle
{
  // Make members accessible for instances of the class
  public int x, y;
  public int GetArea() { return x * y; }
}
```

The member access operator (.) is used after the object's name to reference its accessible members.

```
static void Main()
{
  MyRectangle r = new MyRectangle();
  r.x = 10;
  r.y = 5;
  int a = r.GetArea(); // 50
}
```

Constructor

The class can have a *constructor*. This is a special kind of method used to instantiate (construct) the object. It always has the same name as the class and does not have a return type, because it implicitly returns a new instance of the class. To be accessible from another class it needs to be declared with the public access modifier.

```
public MyRectangle() { x = 10; y = 5; }
```

When a new instance of the class is created, the constructor method is called, which in the example here sets the fields to the specified initial values.

```
static void Main()
{
  MyRectangle r = new MyRectangle(); // calls constructor
}
```

The constructor can have a parameter list, just as any other method. As seen in the following example, this can be used to make the fields' initial values depend on the parameters passed when the object is created.

```
class MyRectangle
{
  public int x, y;

  public MyRectangle(int width, int height)
  {
    x = width; y = height;
  }

  static void Main()
  {
    MyRectangle r = new MyRectangle(20, 15);
  }
}
```

This Keyword

Inside the constructor, as well as in other methods belonging to the object, a special keyword called this can be used. This keyword is a reference to the current instance of the class. Suppose, for example, that the constructor's parameters have the same names as the corresponding fields. The fields could then still be accessed by using the this keyword, even though they are overshadowed by the parameters.

```
class MyRectangle
{
  public int x, y;

  public MyRectangle(int x, int y)
  {
    this.x = x; // set field x to parameter x
    this.y = y;
  }
}
```

Constructor Overloading

To support different parameter lists, the constructor can be overloaded. In the next example, the fields will be assigned default values if the class is instantiated without any arguments. With one argument both fields will be set to the specified value, and with two arguments each field will be assigned a separate value. Attempting to create an object with the wrong number of arguments, or with incorrect data types, will result in a compile-time error, just as with any other method.

```
class MyRectangle
{
  public int x, y;
  public MyRectangle() { x = 10; y = 5; }
  public MyRectangle(int a) { x =  a; y = a; }
  public MyRectangle(int a, int b) { x =  a; y = b; }
}
```

Constructor Chaining

The this keyword can also be used to call one constructor from another. This is known as constructor chaining and allows for greater code reuse. Note that the keyword appears as a method call before the constructor body and after a colon.

```
class MyRectangle
{
  public int x, y;
  public MyRectangle() : this(10,5) {}
  public MyRectangle(int a) : this(a,a) {}
  public MyRectangle(int a, int b) { x = a; y = b; }
}
```

Initial Field Values

If there are fields in a class that need to be assigned initial values, such as in the previous example, the fields can simply be initialized at the same time as they are declared. This can make the code a bit cleaner. The initial values will be assigned when the object is created, before the constructor is called.

```
class MyRectangle
{
  public int x = 10, y = 20;
}
```

An assignment of this type is called a *field initializer*. Such an assignment cannot refer to another instance field.

Default Constructor

It is possible to create a class even if no constructors are defined. This is because the compiler will automatically add a default parameterless constructor to such a class. The default constructor will instantiate the object and set each field to its default value.

```
class MyRectangle {}
class MyApp
{
  static void Main()
  {
    // Calls default constructor
    MyRectangle r = new MyRectangle();
  }
}
```

Object Initializers

When creating an object, as of C# 3.0, it is possible to initialize the object's public fields within the instantiation statement. A code block is then added, containing a comma-separated list of field assignments. This object initializer block will be processed after the constructor has been called.

```
class MyRectangle
{
  public int x, y;
}
class MyClass
{
  static void Main()
  {
    // Use object initializer
    MyRectangle r = new MyRectangle() { x = 10, y = 5 };
  }
}
```

If there are no arguments for the constructor, the parentheses may be removed.

```
MyRectangle r = new MyRectangle { x = 10, y = 5 };
```

Partial Class

A class definition can be split up into separate source files by using the partial type modifier. These partial classes will be combined into the final type by the compiler. All parts of a partial class must have the partial keyword and share the same access level.

```
// File1.cs
public partial class MyPartialClass {}
```

```
// File2.cs
public partial class MyPartialClass {}
```

Splitting classes across multiple source files is primarily useful when part of a class is generated automatically. For example, this feature is used by Visual Studio's graphical user interface builder to separate automatically generated code from user-defined code. Partial classes can also make it easier for multiple programmers to work on the same class simultaneously.

Garbage Collector

The .NET Framework has a garbage collector that periodically releases memory used by objects when they are no longer accessible. This frees the programmer from the often tedious and error-prone task of manual memory management. An object will be eligible for destruction when there are no more references to it. This occurs, for example, when a local object variable goes out of scope. Bear in mind that an object cannot be explicitly deallocated in C#.

```
static void Main()
{
  if (true) {
   string s = "";
  }
  // String object s becomes inaccessible here and will be
  destroyed
}
```

Destructor

In addition to constructors, a class can also have a destructor. The destructor is used to release any unmanaged resources allocated by the object. It is called automatically before an object is destroyed and cannot be called explicitly. The name of the destructor is the same as the class name, but preceded by a tilde (~). A class may only have one destructor and it does not take any parameters or return any value.

```csharp
class MyComponent
{
  public System.ComponentModel.Component comp;

  public MyComponent()
  {
    comp = new System.ComponentModel.Component();
  }

  // Destructor
  ~MyComponent()
  {
    comp.Dispose();
  }
}
```

In general, the .NET Framework garbage collector automatically manages the allocation and release of memory for objects. However, when a class uses unmanaged resources—such as files, network connections, and user interface components—a destructor should be used to free up those resources when they are no longer needed.

Null Keyword

The null keyword is used to represent a null reference, which is a reference that does not refer to any object. It can only be assigned to variables of reference type, and not to value type variables.

```csharp
string s = null;
```

Trying to access members of an object referring to null will cause an exception, because there is no valid instance to dereference.

```
int length = s.Length; // error: NullReferenceException
```

In order to safely access instance members of an object that may be null, a check for a null reference should first be carried out. This test can be done for instance using the equal to operator (==).

```
class MyApp
{
  public string s; // null by default

  static void Main()
  {
    MyApp o = new MyApp();
    if (o.s == null) { o.s = ""; } // create a valid object
(empty string)
    int length = o.s.Length; // 0
  }
}
```

Another option is to use the ternary operator to assign a suitable value in case a null string is encountered.

```
string s = null;
int length = (s != null) ? s.Length : 0; // 0
```

Nullable Types

A value type can be made to hold the value null in addition to its normal range of values by appending a question mark (?) to its underlying type. This is called a *nullable type* and allows the simple types, as well as other struct types, to indicate an undefined value. For example, bool? is a nullable type that can hold the values true, false, and null.

```
bool? b = null; // nullable bool type
```

Null-Coalescing Operator

The null-coalescing operator (??) returns the left-hand operand if it is not null and otherwise returns the right-hand operand. This conditional operator provides an easy syntax for assigning a nullable type to a non-nullable type.

```
int? i = null;
int j = i ?? 0; // 0
```

A variable of a nullable type should not be explicitly cast to a non-nullable type. Doing so will cause a runtime error if the variable has null as its value.

```
int? i = null;
int j = (int)i; // error: nullable object must have a value
```

Null-Conditional Operator

In C# 6.0, the null-conditional operator (?.) was introduced. This operator provides a concise way to perform null checks when accessing object members. It works like the regular member access operator (.), except that if a null reference is encountered, the value null is returned instead of causing an exception to occur.

```
string s = null;
int? length = s?.Length; // null
```

Combining this operator with the null-coalescing operator is useful for assigning a default value whenever a null reference appears.

```
string s = null;
int length = s?.Length ?? 0; // 0
```

Another use for the null-conditional operator is together with arrays. The question mark can be placed before the square brackets of the array and the expression will then evaluate to null if the array is uninitialized. Note that this will not check if the array index referenced is out of range.

```
string[] s = null;
string s3 = s?[3]; // null
```

Default Values

The default value of a reference type is null. For the simple data types the default values are as follows: numerical types become 0, a char has the Unicode character for zero (\0000), and a bool is false. Default values will be assigned automatically by the compiler for fields. However, explicitly specifying the default value for fields is considered good programming since it makes the code easier to understand. For local variables the default values will not be set by the compiler. Instead, the compiler forces the programmer to assign values to any local variables that are used, so as to avoid problems associated with using unassigned variables.

```
class MyClass
{
  int x; // field is assigned default value 0

  void test()
  {
    int x; // local variable must be assigned if used
  }
}
```

CHAPTER 11

Inheritance

Inheritance allows a class to acquire the members of another class. In the following example, the class Square inherits from Rectangle, specified by a colon. Rectangle then becomes the base class of Square, which in turn becomes a derived class of Rectangle. In addition to its own members, Square gains all accessible members in Rectangle, except for any constructors or destructors.

```
// Base class (parent class)
class Rectangle
{
  public int x = 10, y = 10;
  public int GetArea() { return x * y; }
}

// Derived class (child class)
class Square : Rectangle {}
```

Object Class

A class in C# may only inherit from one base class. If no base class is specified, the class will implicitly inherit from System.Object. This is therefore the root class of all other classes.

```
class Rectangle : System.Object {}
```

© Mikael Olsson 2018
M. Olsson, *C# 7 Quick Syntax Reference*, https://doi.org/10.1007/978-1-4842-3817-2_11

C# has a unified type system in that all data types, directly or indirectly, inherit from Object. This does not only apply to classes, but also to other data types, such as arrays and simple types. For example, the int keyword is only an alias for the System.Int32 struct type. Likewise, object is an alias for the System.Object class.

```
System.Object o = new object();
```

Because all types inherit from Object, they all share a common set of methods. One such method is ToString, which returns a string representation of the current object. The method often returns the name of the type, which can be useful for debugging purposes.

```
System.Console.WriteLine( o.ToString() ); // "System.Object"
```

Downcast and Upcast

Conceptually, a derived class is a specialization of its base class. This means that Square is a kind of Rectangle as well as an Object, and it can therefore be used anywhere a Rectangle or Object is expected. If an instance of Square is created, it can be upcast to Rectangle since the derived class contains everything in the base class.

```
Square s = new Square();
Rectangle r = s; // upcast
```

The object is now viewed as a Rectangle, so only Rectangle's members can be accessed. When the object is downcast back into a Square, everything specific to the Square class will still be preserved. This is because the Rectangle only contained the Square; it did not change the Square object in any way.

```
Square s2 = (Square)r; // downcast
```

The downcast has to be made explicit since downcasting an actual Rectangle into a Square is not allowed.

```
Rectangle r2 = new Rectangle();
Square s3 = (Square)r2; // error
```

The is and as Keywords

There are two operators that can be used to avoid exceptions when casting objects: is and as. First, the is operator returns true if the left side object can be cast to the right side type without causing an exception.

```
Rectangle q = new Square();
if (q is Square) { Square o = q; } // condition is true
```

The second operator used to avoid object casting exceptions is the as operator. This operator provides an alternative way of writing an explicit cast, with the difference that if it fails, the reference will be set to null.

```
Rectangle r = new Rectangle();
Square o = r as Square; // invalid cast, returns null
```

When using the as operator, there is no distinction between a null value and the wrong type. Furthermore, this operator only works with reference type variables. Pattern matching provides a way to overcome these restrictions.

Pattern Matching

C# 7.0 introduced pattern matching, which extends the use of the is operator to both testing a variable's type and, upon validation, assigning it to a new variable of that type. This provides a new method for safely casting variables between types, and also largely replaces the use of the as operator with the following, more convenient syntax.

```
Rectangle q = new Square();
if (q is Square mySquare) { /* use mySquare here */ }
```

When a pattern variable like mySquare is introduced in an if statement, it also becomes available in the enclosing block's scope. Hence the variable can be used even after the end of the if statement. This is not the case for other conditional or looping statements.

```
object obj = "Hello";
if (!(obj is string text)) { return; } // exit if obj is not a
                                          string
System.Console.WriteLine(text); // "Hello"
```

The extended is expression works not just with reference types, but also with value types. In addition to types, any constant may also be used, as seen in the following example.

```
class MyApp
{
  void Test(object o)
  {
    if (o is 5) System.Console.WriteLine("5");
    else if (o is int i) System.Console.WriteLine("int:" + i);
    else if (o is null) System.Console.WriteLine("null");
  }

  static void Main()
  {
    MyApp c = new MyApp();
    c.Test(5); // "5"
```

```
    c.Test(1); // "int:1"
    c.Test(null); // "null"
  }
}
```

Pattern matching works not only with if statements but also with switch statements, using a slightly different syntax. The type to be matched and any variable to be assigned is placed after the case keyword. The previous example method can be rewritten as follows.

```
void Test(object o)
{
  switch(o)
  {
    case 5: System.Console.WriteLine("5"); break;
    case int i: System.Console.WriteLine("int:" + i); break;
    case null: System.Console.WriteLine("null"); break;
  }
}
```

Note that the order of the case expressions matter when performing pattern matching. The first case matching the number 5 must appear before the more general int case in order for it to be matched.

Boxing

The unified type system of C# allows for a variable of value type to be implicitly converted into a reference type of the Object class. This operation is known as *boxing* and once the value has been copied into the object, it is seen as a reference type.

```
int myInt = 5;
object myObj = myInt; // boxing
```

Unboxing

The opposite of boxing is *unboxing*. This converts the boxed value back into a variable of its value type. The unboxing operation must be explicit. If the object is not unboxed into the correct type, a runtime error will occur.

```
myInt = (int)myObj; // unboxing
```

CHAPTER 12

Redefining Members

A member in a derived class can redefine a member in its base class. This can be done for all kinds of inherited members, but it is most often used to give instance methods new implementations. To give a method a new implementation, the method is redefined in the child class with the same signature as it has in the base class. The signature includes the name, parameters, and return type of the method.

```
class Rectangle
{
  public int x = 1, y = 10;
  public int GetArea() { return x * y; }
}

class Square : Rectangle
{
  public int GetArea() { return 2 * x; }
}
```

Hiding Members

It must be specified whether the method is intended to *hide* or *override* the inherited method. By default, the new method will hide it, but the compiler will give a warning that the behavior should be explicitly specified.

© Mikael Olsson 2018
M. Olsson, *C# 7 Quick Syntax Reference*, https://doi.org/10.1007/978-1-4842-3817-2_12

To remove the warning, the new modifier needs to be used. This specifies that the intention was to hide the inherited method and to replace it with a new implementation.

```
class Square : Rectangle
{
  public new int GetArea() { return 2 * x; }
}
```

Overriding Members

Before a method can be overridden, the virtual modifier must first be added to the method in the base class. This modifier allows the method to be overridden in a derived class.

```
class Rectangle
{
  public int x = 1, y = 10;
  public virtual int GetArea() { return x * y; }
}
```

The override modifier can then be used to change the implementation of the inherited method.

```
class Square : Rectangle
{
  public override int GetArea() { return 2 * x; }
}
```

Hiding and Overriding

The difference between override and new is shown when a Square is upcast to a Rectangle. If the method is redefined with the new modifier then this allows access to the previously hidden method defined in Rectangle. On the other hand, if the method is redefined using the override modifier, then the upcast will still call the version defined in Square. In short, the new modifier redefines the method down the class hierarchy, while override redefines the method both up and down in the hierarchy.

Sealed Keyword

To stop an overridden method from being further overridden in classes that inherit from the derived class, the method can be declared as sealed to negate the virtual modifier.

```
class MyClass
{
  public sealed override int NonOverridable() {}
}
```

A class can also be declared as sealed to prevent any class from inheriting it.

```
sealed class NonInheritable {}
```

Base Keyword

There is a way to access a parent's method even if it has been redefined. This is done by using the base keyword to reference the base class instance. Whether the method is hidden or overridden, it can still be reached by using this keyword.

```
class Triangle : Rectangle
{
  public override GetArea() { return base.GetArea()/2; }
}
```

The base keyword can also be used to call a base class constructor from a derived class constructor. The keyword is then used as a method call before the constructor's body, prefixed by a colon.

```
class Rectangle
{
  public int x = 1, y = 10;
  public Rectangle(int a, int b) { x = a; y = b; }
}

class Square : Rectangle
{
  public Square(int a) : base(a,a) {}
}
```

When a derived class constructor does not have an explicit call to the base class constructor, the compiler will automatically insert a call to the parameterless base class constructor in order to ensure that the base class is properly constructed.

```
class Square : Rectangle
{
  public Square(int a) {} // : base() implicitly added
}
```

Note that if the base class has a constructor defined that is not parameterless, the compiler will not create a default parameterless constructor. Therefore, defining a constructor in the derived class, without an explicit call to a defined base class constructor, will cause a compile-time error.

```
class Base { public Base(int a) {} }
class Derived : Base {} // compile-time error
```

CHAPTER 13

Access Levels

Every class member has an accessibility level that determines where the member will be visible. There are six of them available in C#: `public`, `protected`, `internal`, `protected internal`, `private`, and `private protected`, the last of which was added in C# 7.2. The default access level for members of a class is `private`.

Private Access

All members regardless of access level are accessible in the class in which they are declared, the defining class. This is the only place where a private member can be accessed.

```
public class MyBase
{
  // Unrestricted access
  public int myPublic;

  // Defining assembly or derived class
  protected internal int myProtInt;

 // Derived class within defining assembly
  private protected int myPrivProt;

  // Defining assembly
  internal int myInternal;
```

© Mikael Olsson 2018
M. Olsson, *C# 7 Quick Syntax Reference*, https://doi.org/10.1007/978-1-4842-3817-2_13

```
// Derived class
protected int myProtected;

// Defining class only
private int myPrivate;

void Test()
{
  myPublic    = 0; // allowed
  myProtInt   = 0; // allowed
  myPrivProt  = 0; // allowed
  myInternal  = 0; // allowed
  myProtected = 0; // allowed
  myPrivate   = 0; // allowed
}
}
```

Protected Access

A protected member can be accessed from within a derived class, but it is inaccessible from any other classes.

```
class Derived : MyBase
{
  void Test()
  {
    myPublic    = 0; // allowed
    myProtInt   = 0; // allowed
    myPrivProt  = 0; // allowed
    myInternal  = 0; // allowed
    myProtected = 0; // allowed
    myPrivate   = 0; // inaccessible
  }
}
```

74

Internal Access

An internal member can be accessed anywhere within the local assembly, but not from another assembly. An assembly is the compilation unit of a .NET project, either an executable program (`.exe`) or a library (`.dll`).

```
// Defining assembly
class AnyClass
{
  void Test(MyBase m)
  {
    m.myPublic    = 0; // allowed
    m.myProtInt   = 0; // allowed
    m.myPrivProt  = 0; // inaccessible
    m.myInternal  = 0; // allowed
    m.myProtected = 0; // inaccessible
    m.myPrivate   = 0; // inaccessible
  }
}
```

In Visual Studio, a project (assembly) is contained within a solution. You can add a second project to your solution by right-clicking the Solution node in the Solution Explorer window and selecting Add ➤ New Project.

For the second project to be able to reference public types from the first project, you need to add a reference. To do so, right-click the References node of the second project and click Add Reference. Under Projects, select the name of the first project and click OK to add the reference.

Protected Internal Access

Protected internal access means either protected or internal. A protected internal member can therefore be accessed anywhere within the current assembly, or in classes outside the assembly that are derived from the enclosing class.

```
// Other assembly
class Derived : MyBase
{
  void Test()
  {
    myPublic    = 0; // allowed
    myProtInt   = 0; // allowed
    myPrivProt  = 0; // inaccessible
    myInternal  = 0; // inaccessible
    myProtected = 0; // allowed
    myPrivate   = 0; // inaccessible
  }
}
```

Private Protected Access

A private protected member is accessible only within the defining assembly in types that derive from the defining type. Put another way, this access level restricts the member's visibility to being both protected and internal.

```
// Defining assembly
class Derived : MyBase
{
  void Test()
  {
    myPublic    = 0; // allowed
    myProtInt   = 0; // allowed
    myPrivProt  = 0; // allowed
    myInternal  = 0; // allowed
    myProtected = 0; // allowed
    myPrivate   = 0; // inaccessible
  }
}
```

Public Access

The public modifier gives unrestricted access from anywhere that a member can be referenced.

```
// Other assembly
class AnyClass
{
  void Test(MyBase m)
  {
    m.myPublic    = 0; // allowed
    m.myProtInt   = 0; // inaccessible
    m.myPrivProt  = 0; // inaccessible
    m.myInternal  = 0; // inaccessible
    m.myProtected = 0; // inaccessible
    m.myPrivate   = 0; // inaccessible
  }
}
```

Top-Level Access Levels

A top-level member is a type that is declared outside of any other types.
In C#, the following types can be declared on the top-level: class,
interface, struct, enum, and delegate. By default, these uncontained
members are given internal access. To be able to use a top-level member
from another assembly, that member has to be marked as public.
This is the only other access level allowed for top-level members.

```
internal class MyInternalClass {}
public class MyPublicClass {}
```

Inner Classes

Classes may contain inner classes, which can be set to any one of the
six access levels. The access levels have the same effect on inner classes
as they do on other members. If the class is inaccessible, it cannot be
instantiated or inherited. By default, inner classes are private, which
means that they can only be used within the class where they are defined.

```
class MyBase
{
  // Inner classes (nested classes)
  public class MyPublic {}
  protected internal class MyProtInt {}
  private protected class MyPrivProt {}
  internal class MyInternal {}
  protected class MyProtected {}
  private class MyPrivate {}
}
```

Access Level Guideline

As a guideline, when choosing an access level it is generally best to use the most restrictive level possible. This is because the more places a member can be accessed, the more places it can be accessed incorrectly, which makes the code harder to debug. Using restrictive access levels will also make it easier to modify a class without breaking the code for any other programmers using that class.

CHAPTER 14

Static

The static keyword can be used to declare fields and methods that can be accessed without having to create an instance of the class. Static (class) members only exist in one copy, which belongs to the class itself, whereas instance (non-static) members are created as new copies for each new object. This means that static methods cannot use instance members since these methods are not part of an instance. On the other hand, instance methods can use both static and instance members.

```csharp
class MyCircle
{
  // Instance variable (one per object)
  public float r = 10F;

  // Static/class variable (only one instance)
  public static float pi = 3.14F;

  // Instance method
  public float GetArea()
  {
    return ComputeArea(r);
  }
}
```

© Mikael Olsson 2018
M. Olsson, *C# 7 Quick Syntax Reference*, https://doi.org/10.1007/978-1-4842-3817-2_14

```
// Static/class method
public static float ComputeArea(float a)
{
  return pi*a*a;
}
}
```

Accessing Static Members

To access a static member from outside the class, the class name is used followed by the dot operator. This operator is the same as the one used to access instance members, but to reach them an object reference is required. An object reference cannot be used to access a static member.

```
class MyApp
{
  static void Main()
  {
    float f = MyCircle.ComputeArea(MyCircle.pi);
  }
}
```

Static Methods

The advantage of static members is that they can be used by other classes without having to create an instance of the class. Fields should therefore be declared static when only a single instance of the variable is needed. Methods should be declared static if they perform a generic function that is independent of any instance variables. A good example of this is the System.Math class, which provides a multitude of mathematical methods. This class contains only static members and constants.

```
static void Main()
{
  double pi = System.Math.PI;
}
```

Static Fields

Static fields have the advantage that they persist throughout the life of the application. A static variable can therefore be used, for example, to record the number of times that a method has been called.

```
static int count = 0;
public static void Dummy()
{
  count++;
}
```

The default value for a static field will be set only once before it is first used.

Static Classes

A class can also be marked static if it only contains static members and constant fields. A static class cannot be inherited or instantiated into an object. Attempting to do so will cause a compile-time error.

```
static class MyCircle {}
```

Static Constructor

A static constructor can perform any actions needed to initialize a class. Typically, these actions involve initializing static fields that cannot be initialized as they are declared. This can be necessary if their initialization requires more than one line, or some other logic, to be initialized.

```
class MyClass
{
  static int[] array = new int[5];

  static MyClass()
  {
    for(int i = 0; i < array.Length; i++)
      array[i] = i;
  }
}
```

The static constructor, in contrast to the regular instance constructor, will only be run once. This occurs automatically, either when an instance of the class is created or when a static member of the class is referenced. Static constructors cannot be called directly and are not inherited. In case the static fields also have initializers, those initial values will be assigned before the static constructor is run.

Extension Methods

A new feature in C# 3.0 is extension methods, which provide a way to seemingly add new instance methods to an existing class outside its definition. An extension method must be defined as static in a static class and the keyword this is used on the first parameter to designate which class to extend.

```
static class MyExtensions
{
  // Extension method
  public static int ToInt(this string s) {
    return Int32.Parse(s);
  }
}
```

The extension method is callable for objects of its first parameter type, in this case string, as if it were an instance method of that class. No reference to the static class is needed.

```
class MyApp
{
  static void Main() {
    string s = "10";
    int i = s.ToInt();
  }
}
```

Because the extension method has an object reference, it can use instance members of the class it is extending. However, it cannot use members of any class that is inaccessible due to its access level. The benefit of extension methods is that they enable you to "add" methods to a class without having to modify or derive the original type.

CHAPTER 15

Properties

Properties in C# provide the ability to protect a field by reading and writing to it through special methods called *accessors*. They are generally declared as public with the same data type as the field they are going to protect, followed by the name of the property and a code block that defines the get and set accessors.

```
class Time
{
  private int seconds;

  public int sec
  {
    get { return seconds; }
    set { seconds = value; }
  }
}
```

Note that the contextual *value* keyword corresponds to the value assigned to the property. Properties are implemented as methods, but used as though they are fields.

```
static void Main()
{
  Time t = new Time();
  t.sec = 5;
  int s = t.sec; // 5
}
```

© Mikael Olsson 2018
M. Olsson, *C# 7 Quick Syntax Reference*, https://doi.org/10.1007/978-1-4842-3817-2_15

Property Advantages

Since there is no special logic in the previously defined property, it is functionally the same as if it had been a public field. However, as a general rule, public fields should never be used in real world programming because of the many advantages that properties bring.

First of all, properties allow developers to change the internal implementation of the property without breaking any programs that are using it. This is of particular importance for published classes, which may be in use by other developers. In the Time class, for example, the field's data type could need to be changed from int to byte. With properties, this conversion could be handled in the background. With a public field, however, changing the underlying data type for a published class will likely break any programs that are using the class.

```
class Time
{
  private byte seconds;

  public int sec
  {
    get
    {
      return (int)seconds;
    }
    set
    {
      seconds = (byte)value;
    }
  }
}
```

A second advantage of properties is that they allow the data to be validated before permitting a change. For example, the seconds field can be prevented from being assigned a negative value in the following way.

```
class Time
{
  private int seconds;

  get { return seconds; }
  set
  {
    if (value > 0)
      seconds = value;
    else
      seconds = 0;
  }
}
```

Properties do not have to correspond to an actual field. They can just as well compute their own values. The data could even come from outside the class, such as from a database. There is also nothing that prevents the programmer from doing other things in the accessors, such as keeping an update counter.

```
public int hour
{
  get
  {
    return seconds / 3600;
  }
```

```
  set
  {
    seconds = value * 3600;
    count++;
  }
}

private int count = 0;
```

Read-Only and Write-Only Properties

Either one of the accessors can be left out. Without the set accessor, the property becomes read-only, and by leaving out the get accessor instead, the property is made write-only.

```
// Read-only property
private int sec
{
  public get { return seconds; }
}
// Write-only property
private int sec
{
  public set { seconds = value; }
}
```

Property Access Levels

The accessor's access levels can be restricted. For instance, to prevent a property from being modified from outside the class, the set accessor can be made private.

```
private set { seconds = value; }
```

The access level of the property itself can also be changed to restrict both accessors. By default, the accessors are public and the property itself is private.

```
private int sec { get; set; }
```

Auto-Implemented Properties

The kind of property where the get and set accessors directly correspond to a field is very common. Because of this, there is a shorthand way of writing such a property, by leaving out the accessor code blocks and the private field. This syntax was introduced in C# 3.0 and is called an auto-implemented property.

```
class Time
{
  public int sec { get; set; }
}
```

Two additional capabilities were added to auto-properties in C# 6. First, an initial value can be set as part of the declaration. Second, an auto-property can be made read-only by leaving out the set accessor. Such a property can only be set in the constructor, or as part of the declaration, as shown here.

```
class Time
{
  // Read-only auto-property with initializer
  public System.DateTime Created { get; } = System.DateTime.Now;
}
```

CHAPTER 16

Indexers

Indexers allow an object to be treated as an array. They are declared in the same way as properties, except that the this keyword is used instead of a name and their accessors take parameters. In the following example, the indexer corresponds to an object array called data, so the type of the indexer is set to object.

```
class MyArray
{
  object[] data = new object[10];

  public object this[int i]
  {
    get { return data[i]; }
    set { data[i] = value; }
  }
}
```

The get accessor returns the specified element from the object array, and the set accessor inserts the value into the specified element. With the indexer in place an instance of this class can be created and used as an array, both to get and set the elements.

```
static void Main()
{
  MyArray a = new MyArray();
  a[5] = "Hello World";
  object o = a[5]; // Hello World
}
```

Indexer Parameters

The parameter list of an indexer is similar to that of a method, except that it must have at least one parameter and the ref or out modifiers are not allowed. For example, if there is a two-dimensional array, the column and row indexes can be passed as separate parameters.

```
class MyArray
{
  object[,] data = new object[10,10];

  public object this[int i, int j]
  {
    get { return data[i,j]; }
    set { data[i,j] = value; }
  }
}
```

The index parameter does not have to be of an integer type. An object can just as well be passed as the index parameter. The get accessor can then be used to return the index position where the passed object is located.

```
class MyArray
{
  object[] data = new object[10];

  public int this[object o]
  {
    get { return System.Array.IndexOf(data, o); }
  }
}
```

Indexer Overloading

Both of these functionalities can be provided by overloading the indexer. The type and number of arguments will then determine which indexer gets called.

```
class MyArray
{
  object[] data = new object[10];

  public int this[object o]
  {
    get { return System.Array.IndexOf(data, o); }
  }

  public object this[int i]
  {
    get { return data[i]; }
    set { data[i] = value; }
  }
}
```

Keep in mind that in a real program a range check should be included in the accessors, so as to avoid exceptions caused by trying to go beyond the length of the array.

```
public object this[int i]
{
  get
  {
    return (i >= 0 && i < data.Length) ? data[i] : null;
  }
  set
  {
    if (i >= 0 && i < data.Length)
      data[i] = value;
  }
}
```

CHAPTER 17

Interfaces

An interface is used to specify members that deriving classes must implement. They are defined with the `interface` keyword followed by a name and a code block. Their naming convention is to start with a capital I and then to have each word initially capitalized.

```
interface IMyInterface {}
```

Interface Signatures

The interface code block can only contain signatures, and only those of methods, properties, indexers, and events. The interface members cannot have any implementations. Instead, their bodies are replaced by semicolons. They also cannot have any access modifiers since interface members are always public.

```
interface IMyInterface
{
  // Interface method
  int GetArea();

  // Interface property
  int Area { get; set; }
```

© Mikael Olsson 2018
M. Olsson, *C# 7 Quick Syntax Reference*, https://doi.org/10.1007/978-1-4842-3817-2_17

```
// Interface indexer
int this[int index] { get; set; }

// Interface event
event System.EventHandler MyEvent;
}
```

Interface Example

In the following example, an interface called IComparable is defined with a single method named Compare.

```
interface IComparable
{
  int Compare(object o);
}
```

The class Circle defined next implements this interface, by using the same notation as is used for inheritance. The Circle class must then define the Compare method, which for this class will return the difference between the circle radiuses. The implemented member must be public, in addition to having the same signature as the one defined in the interface.

```
class Circle : IComparable
{
  int r;

  public int Compare(object o)
  {
    return r - (o as Circle).r;
  }
}
```

Although a class can only inherit from one base class, it may implement any number of interfaces. It does so by specifying the interfaces in a comma-separated list after the base class.

Functionality Interface

IComparable demonstrates the first use of interfaces, which is to define a specific functionality that classes can share. It allows programmers to use the interface members without having to know the actual type of a class. To illustrate, the following method takes two IComparable objects and returns the largest one. This method will work for any two objects of the same class that implement the IComparable interface, because the method only uses the functionality exposed through that interface.

```
static object Largest(IComparable a, IComparable b)
{
   return (a.Compare(b) > 0) ? a : b;
}
```

Class Interface

A second way to use an interface is to provide an actual interface for a class, through which the class can be used. Such an interface defines the functionality that programmers using the class will need.

```
interface IMyClass
{
   void Exposed();
}
```

```
class MyClass : IMyClass
{
  public void Exposed() {}
  public void Hidden()   {}
}
```

The programmers can then view instances of the class through this interface, by enclosing the objects in variables of the interface type.

```
IMyInterface m = new MyClass();
```

This abstraction provides two benefits. First, it makes it easier for other programmers to use the class since they now only have access to the members that are relevant to them. Second, it makes the class more flexible since its implementation can change without being noticeable by other programmers using the class, as long as the interface is followed.

CHAPTER 18

Abstract

An abstract class provides a partial implementation that other classes can build on. When a class is declared as abstract, it means that the class can contain incomplete members that must be implemented in derived classes, in addition to normal class members.

Abstract Members

Any member that requires a body can be declared abstract—such as methods, properties, and indexers. These members are then left unimplemented and only specify their signatures, while their bodies are replaced with semicolons.

```
abstract class Shape
{
  // Abstract method
  public abstract int GetArea();

  // Abstract property
  public abstract int area { get; set; }

  // Abstract indexer
  public abstract int this[int index] { get; set; }

  // Abstract event
  public delegate void MyDelegate();
```

© Mikael Olsson 2018
M. Olsson, *C# 7 Quick Syntax Reference*, https://doi.org/10.1007/978-1-4842-3817-2_18

```
public abstract event MyDelegate MyEvent;

// Abstract class
public abstract class InnerShape {};
}
```

Abstract Example

In the following example, the class has an abstract method named GetArea.

```
abstract class Shape
{
  private int x = 100, y = 100;
  public abstract int GetArea();
}
```

If a class derives from this abstract class, it is then forced to override the abstract member. This is different from the virtual modifier, which specifies that the member may optionally be overridden.

```
class Rectangle : Shape
{
  public int GetArea() { return x * y; }
}
```

The deriving class can be declared abstract as well, in which case it does not have to implement any of the abstract members.

```
abstract class Rectangle : Shape {}
```

An abstract class can also inherit from a non-abstract class.

```
class NonAbstract {}
abstract class Abstract : NonAbstract {}
```

If the base class has virtual members, these can be overridden as abstract to force further deriving classes to provide new implementations for them.

```
class MyClass
{
  void virtual Dummy() {}
}

abstract class Abstract : MyClass
{
  void abstract override Dummy() {}
}
```

An abstract class can be used as an interface to hold objects made from derived classes.

```
Shape s = new Rectangle();
```

It is not possible to instantiate an abstract class. Even so, an abstract class may have constructors that can be called from derived classes by using the base keyword.

```
Shape s = new Shape(); // compile-time error
```

Abstract Classes and Interfaces

Abstract classes are similar to interfaces in many ways. Both can define member signatures that deriving classes must implement, yet neither one of them can be instantiated. The key differences are first that the abstract class can contain non-abstract members, while the interface cannot. And second, a class can implement any number of interfaces but only inherit from one class, abstract or not.

```
// Defines default functionality and definitions
abstract class Shape
{
  public int x = 100, y = 100;
  public abstract int GetArea();
}
class Rectangle : Shape {} // class is a Shape

// Defines an interface or a specific functionality
interface IComparable
{
  int Compare(object o);
}
class MyClass : IComparable {} // class can be compared
```

An abstract class, just like a non-abstract class, can extend one base class and implement any number of interfaces. An interface, however, cannot inherit from a class. It can inherit from another interface, which effectively combines the two interfaces into one.

CHAPTER 19

Namespaces

Namespaces provide a way to group related top-level members into a hierarchy. They are also used to avoid naming conflicts. A top-level member, such as a class, that is not included in a namespace is said to belong to the default namespace. It can be moved to another namespace by being enclosed in a namespace block. The naming convention for namespaces is the same as for classes, with each word initially capitalized.

```
namespace MyNamespace
{
  class MyClass {}
}
```

Nested Namespaces

Namespaces can be nested any number of levels deep to further define the namespace hierarchy.

```
namespace MyNamespace
{
  namespace NestedNamespace
  {
    class MyClass {}
  }
}
```

© Mikael Olsson 2018
M. Olsson, *C# 7 Quick Syntax Reference*, https://doi.org/10.1007/978-1-4842-3817-2_19

A more concise way to write this is to separate the namespaces with a dot.

```
namespace MyNamespace.NestedNamespace
{
  class MyClass {}
}
```

Note that declaring the same namespace again in another class within the project has the same effect as if both namespaces were included in the same block, even if the class is located in another source code file.

Namespace Access

To access a class from another namespace, you need to specify its fully qualified name.

```
namespace MyNamespace.NestedNamespace
{
  public class MyClass {}
}

namespace OtherNamespace
{
  class MyApp
  {
    static void Main()
    {
      MyNamespace.NestedNamespace.MyClass myClass;
    }
  }
}
```

Using Directive

The fully qualified name can be shortened by including the namespace with a using directive. The members of that namespace can then be accessed anywhere in the code file without having to prepend the namespace to every reference. It is mandatory to place using directives before all other members in the code file.

```
using MyNamespace.NestedNamespace;
```

Having direct access to these members means that if there is a conflicting member signature in the current namespace, the member in the included namespace will be hidden. For example, if there is a MyClass in the OtherNamespace as well, that class will be used by default. To use the class in the included namespace, the fully qualified name would again have to be specified.

```
using MyNamespace.NestedNamespace;

namespace MyNamespace.NestedNamespace
{
  public class MyClass
  {
    public static int x;
  }
}

namespace OtherNamespace
{
  public class MyClass
  {
    static void Main()
```

```
    {
        int x = MyNamespace.NestedNamespace.MyClass.x;
    }
  }
}
```

To simplify this reference, the using directive can instead be changed to assign the namespace to an alias.

```
using MyAlias = MyNamespace.NestedNamespace;
// ...
int x = MyAlias.MyClass.x;
```

An even shorter way would be to define the fully qualified class name as a new type for the code file, by using the same alias notation.

```
using MyType = MyNamespace.NestedNamespace.MyClass;
// ...
int x = MyType.x;
```

A using static directive was added in C# 6. This directive imports only the accessible static members of the type into the current namespace. In the following example, static members of the Math class can be used without qualification due to the using static directive.

```
using static System.Math;

public class Circle
{
  public double radius { get; set; }
  public double Area
  {
    get { return PI * Pow(radius, 2); }
  }
}
```

CHAPTER 20

Enum

An *enumeration* is a special kind of value type consisting of a list of named constants. To create one, you use the enum keyword followed by a name and a code block containing a comma-separated list of constant elements.

```
enum State { Run, Wait, Stop };
```

This enumeration type can be used to create variables that can hold these constants. To assign a value to the enum variable, the elements are accessed from the enum as if they were static members of a class.

```
State s = State.Run;
```

Enum Example

The switch statement provides a good example of when an enumeration can be useful. Compared to using ordinary constants, an enumeration has the advantage of allowing the programmer to clearly specify what constant values are allowed. This provides compile-time type safety, and IntelliSense also makes the values easier to remember.

```
switch (s)
{
  case State.Run:  break;
  case State.Wait: break;
  case State.Stop: break;
}
```

© Mikael Olsson 2018
M. Olsson, *C# 7 Quick Syntax Reference*, https://doi.org/10.1007/978-1-4842-3817-2_20

Enum Constant Values

There is usually no need to know the actual constant values that the enum constants represent, but sometimes it can be useful. By default, the first element has the value 0, and each successive element has one value higher.

```
enum State
{
  Run,  // 0
  Wait, // 1
  Stop  // 2
};
```

These default values can be overridden by assigning values to the constants. The values can be computed from an expression and they do not have to be unique.

```
enum State
{
  Run = 0, Wait = 3, Stop = Wait + 1
};
```

Enum Constant Type

The underlying type of the constant elements is implicitly specified as int, but this can be changed by using a colon after the enumeration's name followed by the desired integer type.

```
enum MyEnum : byte {};
```

Enum Access Levels and Scope

The access levels for enumerations are the same as for classes. They are internal by default, but can also be declared as public. Although enumerations are usually defined at the top-level, they may be contained within a class. In a class they have private access by default, and can be set to any one of the access levels.

Enum Methods

An enumeration constant can be cast to an int and the ToString method can be used to obtain its name.

```
static void Main()
{
  State s = State.Run;
  int i = (int)s; // 0
  string t = s.ToString(); // Run
}
```

Several enumeration methods are available in the System.Enum class, such as GetNames() to obtain an array containing the names of the enum constants. Note that this method takes a type object (System.Type) as its argument, which is retrieved using the typeof operator.

```
enum Colors { Red, Green };
static void Main()
{
  foreach (string s in System.Enum.GetNames(typeof(Colors)))
  {
    System.Console.Write(s); // "RedGreen"
  }
}
```

111

CHAPTER 21

Exception Handling

Exception handling allows programmers to deal with unexpected situations that may occur in programs. As an example, consider opening a file using the StreamReader class in the System.IO namespace. To see what kinds of exceptions this class may throw, you can hover the cursor over the class name in Visual Studio. For instance, you may see the System.IO exceptions FileNotFoundException and DirectoryNotFoundException. If any of those exceptions occurs, the program will terminate with an error message.

```
using System;
using System.IO;

class ErrorHandling
{
  static void Main()
  {
    // Run-time error
    StreamReader sr = new StreamReader("missing.txt");
  }
}
```

© Mikael Olsson 2018
M. Olsson, *C# 7 Quick Syntax Reference*, https://doi.org/10.1007/978-1-4842-3817-2_21

Try-Catch Statement

To avoid crashing the program the exceptions must be caught using a try-catch statement. This statement consists of a try block containing the code that may cause the exception, and one or more catch clauses. If the try block successfully executes, the program will then continue running after the try-catch statement. However, if an exception occurs, the execution will then be passed to the first catch block able to handle that exception type.

```
try
{
   StreamReader sr = new StreamReader("missing.txt");
}
catch
{
   Console.WriteLine("File not found");
}
```

Catch Block

Since the previous catch block is not set to handle any specific exception, it will catch all of them. This is equivalent to catching the System. Exception class, because all exceptions derive from this class.

```
catch (Exception) {}
```

To catch a more specific exception, that catch block needs to be placed before more general exceptions.

```
catch (FileNotFoundException) {}
catch (Exception) {}
```

The catch block can optionally define an exception object that can be used to obtain more information about the exception, such as a description of the error.

```
catch (Exception e)
{
  Console.WriteLine("Error: " + e.Message);
}
```

Exception Filters

Exception filters were added in C# 6 and allow catch blocks to include conditions. The condition is appended to the catch block using the when keyword. A matched exception will then only be caught if the condition evaluates to true, as in the following example.

```
try
{
  StreamReader sr = new StreamReader("missing.txt");
}
catch (FileNotFoundException e)
when (e.FileName.Contains(".txt"))
{
  Console.WriteLine("Missing text file: " + e.FileName);
}
```

When using exception filters the same exception type may appear in multiple catch clauses. Additionally, there are scenarios when a more general exception can be placed before more specific ones. In the next example, all exceptions are logged by calling a logging method as an exception filter. Because the method returns false, the general exception is not caught and thereby allows for another catch block to handle the exception.

```csharp
using System;
using System.IO;

static class ErrorHandling
{
  // Extension method
  public static bool LogException(this Exception e)
  {
    Console.Error.WriteLine($"Exception: {e}");
    return false;
  }

  static void Main()
  {
    try
    {
      var sr = new StreamReader("missing.txt");
    }
    catch (Exception e) when (LogException(e))
    {
      // Never reached
    }
    catch (FileNotFoundException)
    {
      // Actual handling of exception
    }
  }
}
```

Note the use of the var keyword here, which lets the compiler determine the type of a local variable based on the assignment. In cases like this, when the type of the variable is obvious from the assignment, var can be used to shorten the code and arguably improve readability. When you're not sure what type a variable is, you can hover the mouse cursor over it in the IDE to display the type. Keep in mind that var can only be used when a local variable is both declared and initialized at the same time.

Finally Block

As the last clause in the try-catch statement, a finally block can be added. This block is used to clean up certain resources allocated in the try block. Typically, limited system resources and graphical components need to be released in this way once they are no longer needed. The code in the finally block will always execute, whether or not there is an exception. This will be the case even if the try block ends with a jump statement, such as return.

In the example used previously, the file opened in the try block should be closed if it was successfully opened. This is done properly in the next code segment. To be able to access the StreamReader object from the finally clause, it must be declared outside of the try block. Keep in mind that if you forget to close the stream, the garbage handler will eventually close it for you, but it is good practice to do it yourself.

```
StreamReader sr = null;

try
{
  sr = new StreamReader("missing.txt");
}
catch (FileNotFoundException) {}
finally
{
  if (sr != null) sr.Close();
}
```

The previous statement is known as a `try-catch-finally` statement. The `catch` block may also be left out to create a `try-finally` statement. This statement will not catch any exceptions. Instead, it will ensure the proper disposal of any resources allocated in the `try` block. This can be useful if the allocated resource does not throw any exceptions. For instance, such a class would be `Bitmap`, in the `System.Drawing` namespace.

```
using System.Drawing;
// ...
Bitmap b = null;
try
{
  b = new Bitmap(100, 100);
  System.Console.WriteLine("Width: "   + b.Width + ",
                           Height: " + b.Height);
}
finally
{
  if (b != null) b.Dispose();
}
```

Note that when using a Console Project a reference to the `System.Drawing` assembly needs to be manually added for those members to be accessible. To do so, right-click the References folder in the Solution Explorer window and select Add Reference. Then from Assemblies ➤ Framework, select the `System.Drawing` assembly and click OK to add its reference to your project.

The using Statement

The `using` statement provides a simpler syntax for writing the `try-finally` statement. This statement starts with the `using` keyword followed by the resource to be acquired, specified in parentheses. It then includes a code block in which the obtained resource can be used. When the code block finishes executing, the Dispose method of the object is automatically called to clean it up. This method comes from the System.IDisposable interface, so the specified resource must implement this interface. The following code performs the same function as the one in the previous example, but with fewer lines of code.

```
using System.Drawing;
// ...
using (Bitmap b = new Bitmap(100, 100))
{
  System.Console.WriteLine("Width: "  + b.Width + ",
                          Height: " + b.Height);
}
```

Throwing Exceptions

When a situation occurs that a method cannot recover from, it can generate an exception to signal the caller that the method has failed. This is done using the throw keyword followed by a new instance of a class deriving from System.Exception.

```
static void MakeError()
{
  throw new System.DivideByZeroException("My Error");
}
```

The exception will then propagate up the caller stack until it is caught. If a caller catches the exception but is not able to recover from it, the exception can be rethrown using only the throw keyword. If there are no more try-catch statements, the program will stop executing and display the error message.

```csharp
static void Main()
{
  try { MakeError(); } catch { throw; }
}
```

As a statement, the throw keyword cannot be used in contexts that require an expression, such as inside a ternary statement. C# 7.0 changed this by allowing throw to also be used as an expression. This expands the locations from which exceptions may be thrown, such as inside the following null coalescing expression.

```csharp
using System;
class MyClass
{
  private string _name;
  public string name
  {
    get => _name;
    set => _name = value ?? throw new
      ArgumentNullException(nameof(name)+" was null");
  }

  static void Main()
  {
    MyClass c = new MyClass();
    c.name = null; // exception: name was null
  }
}
```

Note the use of the nameof expression here, which was introduced in C# 6. This expression turns the symbol inside the parentheses into a string. The benefit of this shows itself if the property is renamed, as the IDE can then find and rename this symbol. This would not be the case if a string had been used instead.

CHAPTER 22

Operator Overloading

Operator overloading allows operators to be redefined and used where one or both of the operands are of a certain class. When done correctly, this can simplify the code and make user-defined types as easy to use as the simple types.

Operator Overloading Example

In this example, there is a class called MyNum with an integer field and a constructor for setting that field. There is also a static Add method that adds two MyNum objects together and returns the result as a new MyNum object.

```
class MyNum
{
  public int val;
  public MyNum(int i) { val = i; }
  public static MyNum Add(MyNum a, MyNum b) {
    return new MyNum(a.val + b.val);
  }
}
```

Two MyNum instances can be added together using the Add method.

```
MyNum a = new MyNum(10), b = new MyNum(5);
MyNum c = MyNum.Add(a, b);
```

© Mikael Olsson 2018
M. Olsson, *C# 7 Quick Syntax Reference*, https://doi.org/10.1007/978-1-4842-3817-2_22

Binary Operator Overloading

What operator overloading does is simplify this syntax and thereby provide a more intuitive interface for the class. To convert the Add method to an overload method for the addition sign, replace the name of the method with the operator keyword followed by the operator that is to be overloaded. The whitespace between the keyword and the operator can optionally be left out. Note that for an operator overloading method to work, it must be defined as both public and static.

```
class MyNum
{
  public int val;
  public MyNum(int i) { val = i; }
  public static MyNum operator +(MyNum a, MyNum b) {
    return new MyNum(a.val + b.val);
  }
}
```

Since the class now overloads the addition sign, this operator can be used to perform the required calculation.

```
MyNum a = new MyNum(10), b = new MyNum(5);
MyNum c = a + b;
```

Unary Operator Overloading

Addition is a binary operator, because it takes two operands. To overload a unary operator, such as increment (++), a single method parameter is used instead.

```
public static MyNum operator ++(MyNum a)
{
  return new MyNum(a.val + 1);
}
```

Note that this will overload both the postfix and prefix versions of the increment operator.

```
MyNum a = new MyNum(10);
a++;
++a;
```

Return Types and Parameters

When overloading a unary operator, the return type and parameter type must be of the enclosing type. On the other hand, when overloading most binary operators, the return type can be anything, except for void, and only one of the parameters must be of the enclosing type. This means that it is possible to further overload a binary operator with other method parameters, for example to allow a MyNum and an int to be added together.

```
public static MyNum operator +(MyNum a, int b)
{
  return new MyNum(a.val + b);
}
```

Overloadable Operators

C# allows overloading of almost all operators, as can be seen in the following table. The combined assignment operators cannot be explicitly overloaded. Instead, they are implicitly overloaded when their corresponding arithmetic or bitwise operators are overloaded.

Binary Operators	Unary Operators	Not Overloadable
+ - * / % (+= -= *= /= %=) &	^ << >> (&= |= ^= <<= >>=) == != > < >= <=	+ - ! ~ ++ -- true false	&& || = . [ ] ( ) :: ?: ?? -> => new as is sizeof typeof nameof

The comparison operators, as well as true and false, must be overloaded in pairs. For example, overloading the equal operator means that the not equal operator also has to be overloaded.

True and False Operator Overloading

Notice in the previous table that true and false are considered to be operators. By overloading them, objects of a class can be used in conditional statements where the object needs to be evaluated as a Boolean type. When overloading them, the return types must be bool.

```
class MyNum
{
  public int val;
  public MyNum(int i) { val = i; }
  public static bool operator true(MyNum a) {
    return (a.val != 0);
  }
  public static bool operator false(MyNum a) {
    return (a.val == 0);
  }
}
```

```
class MyApp
{
  static void Main() {
    MyNum a = new MyNum(10);
    if (a) System.Console.Write("true");
    else System.Console.Write("false");
  }
}
```

CHAPTER 23

Custom Conversions

This chapter covers how to define custom type conversions for an object. As seen in the following example, a class called MyNum is created with a single int field and a constructor. With a custom type conversion, it becomes possible to allow an int to be implicitly converted to an object of this class.

```
class MyNum
{
  public int val;
  public MyNum(int i) { val = i; }
}
```

Implicit Conversion Methods

For this to work, an implicit conversion method needs to be added to the class. This method's signature looks similar to that used for unary operator overloading. It must be declared as public static and includes the operator keyword. However, instead of an operator symbol the return type is specified, which is the target type for the conversion. The single parameter will hold the value that is to be converted. The implicit keyword is also included, which specifies that the method is used to perform implicit conversions.

© Mikael Olsson 2018
M. Olsson, *C# 7 Quick Syntax Reference*, https://doi.org/10.1007/978-1-4842-3817-2_23

```
public static implicit operator MyNum(int a)
{
  return new MyNum(a);
}
```

With this method in place, an int can be implicitly converted to a MyNum object.

```
MyNum a = 5; // implicit conversion
```

Another conversion method can be added that handles conversions in the opposite direction, from a MyNum object to an int.

```
public static implicit operator int(MyNum a)
{
  return a.val;
}
```

Explicit Conversion Methods

To prevent potentially unintended object type conversions by the compiler, the conversion method can be declared as explicit instead of implicit.

```
public static explicit operator int(MyNum a)
{
  return a.val;
}
```

The explicit keyword means that the programmer has to specify an explicit cast in order to invoke the type conversion method. In particular, explicit conversion methods should be used if the result of the conversion leads to loss of information, or if the conversion method may throw exceptions.

```
MyNum a = 5;
int i = (int)a; // explicit conversion
```

128

CHAPTER 24

Struct

The struct keyword in C# is used to create value types. A struct is similar to a class in that it represents a structure with mainly field and method members. However, a struct is a value type, whereas a class is a reference type. Therefore, a struct variable directly stores the data of the struct, while a class variable only stores a reference to an object allocated in memory.

Struct Variable

Structs share most of the same syntax as classes. For example, the following struct is named Point and consists of two public fields.

```
struct Point
{
  public int x, y;
}
```

Given this struct definition, a variable of the Point type can be initialized in the familiar way using the new operator.

```
Point p = new Point();
```

When creating a struct variable in this way, the default constructor will be called, which sets the fields to their default value. Unlike classes, structs can also be instantiated without using the new operator. The fields

© Mikael Olsson 2018
M. Olsson, *C# 7 Quick Syntax Reference*, https://doi.org/10.1007/978-1-4842-3817-2_24

will then remain unassigned. However, similar to when attempting to use a local uninitialized variable, the compiler will not allow the fields to be read until they have been initialized.

```
Point q;
int y = q.x; // compile-time error
```

Struct Constructors

Structs can contain the same members that classes can, except that they cannot contain destructors or parameterless constructors. The parameterless constructor is automatically provided and may not be user-defined. However, a struct may declare constructors that have parameters. The compiler will then enforce that all struct fields are assigned in the constructors, so as to avoid problems associated with unassigned variables.

```
struct Point
{
  public int x, y;
  public Point(int x, int y)
  {
    this.x = x;
    this.y = y;
  }
}
```

Given this definition, the following statements will both create a Point with the fields initialized to zero.

```
Point p1 = new Point();
Point p2 = new Point(0, 0);
```

Struct Field Initializers

Fields within a struct cannot be given initial values, unless they are declared as const or static.

```
struct Point
{
  public int x = 1, y = 1; // compile-time error
  public static int myStatic = 5; // allowed
  public const int myConst = 10; // allowed
}
```

Struct Inheritance

A struct cannot inherit from another struct or class, and it cannot be a base class. This also means that struct members cannot be declared as protected, private protected, or protected internal, and that struct methods cannot be marked as virtual. Structs implicitly inherit from System.ValueType, which in turn inherits from System.Object. Although structs do not support user-defined inheritance, they can implement interfaces in the same way as classes.

Struct Guideline

The struct type is typically used to represent lightweight classes that encapsulate small groups of related variables. The primary reason for using a struct instead of a class is to get value type semantics. For example, the simple types are in fact all struct types. For these types, it is more natural that assignment copies the value rather than the reference.

Structs can also be useful for performance reasons. A struct is more efficient than a class in terms of memory. It not only takes up less memory than a class, but it also does not need memory to be allocated for it as required by reference type objects. Furthermore, a class requires two memory spaces, one for the variable and one for the object, whereas a struct only needs one. This can make a significant difference for a program that operates on a great number of data structures. Bear in mind that assignment and parameter passing by value are typically more expensive with structs than with reference types, because the entire struct needs to be copied for such operations.

CHAPTER 25

Preprocessors

C# includes a set of preprocessor directives that are mainly used for conditional compilation. Although the C# compiler does not have a separate preprocessor, as C and C++ compilers, the directives shown here are processed as if there were one. That is, they appear to be processed before the actual compilation takes place.

Directive	Description
#if	If
#elif	Else if
#else	Else
#endif	End if
#define	Symbol define
#undef	Symbol undefine
#error	Generate error
#warning	Generate warning
#line	Set line number
#region	Mark section start
#endregion	Mark section end

© Mikael Olsson 2018
M. Olsson, *C# 7 Quick Syntax Reference*, https://doi.org/10.1007/978-1-4842-3817-2_25

Preprocessor Syntax

The preprocessor directives are easily distinguished from normal programming code in that they start with a hash sign (#). They must always occupy a line that is separate from anything else, except for single-line comments. Whitespace may optionally be included before and after the hash mark.

```
#line 1 // set line number
```

Conditional Compilation Symbols

A conditional compilation symbol is created using the #define directive followed by the symbol's name. When a symbol is defined, it will then cause a conditional expression using that condition to be evaluated as true. The symbol will remain defined only within the current source file, starting from the line where the symbol is created.

```
#define MySymbol
```

The #undef (undefine) directive can disable a previously defined symbol.

```
#undef MySymbol
```

Conditional Compilation

The #if and #endif directives specify a section of code that will be included or excluded based on a given condition. Most often, this condition will be a conditional compilation symbol.

```
#if MySymbol
 // ...
#endif
```

Just as with the C# if statement, the #if directive can optionally include any number of #elif (else if) directives and one final #else directive. Conditional directives may also be nested within another conditional section. In longer conditionals, it is good practice to add comments to the #endif directives to help keep track of which #if directive they correspond to.

```
#if Professional
  // ...
#elif Advanced || Enterprise
  // ...
#else
  #if Debug
  // ...
  #endif // Debug
#endif // Professional
```

Diagnostic Directives

There are two diagnostic directives: #error and #warning. The #error directive is used to abort a compilation by generating a compilation error. This directive can optionally take a parameter that provides an error description.

```
#if Professional && Enterprise
 #error Build cannot be both Professional and Enterprise
#endif
```

Similar to error, the #warning directive generates a compilation warning message. This directive will not stop the compilation.

```
#if !Professional && !Enterprise
 #warning Build should be Professional or Enterprise
#endif
```

Line Directive

Another directive that affects the compiler's output is #line. This directive is used to change the line number and optionally the source filename that is displayed when an error or warning occurs during compilation. This is mainly useful when using a program that combines the source files into an intermediate file, which is then compiled.

```
#line 500 "MyFile"
#error MyError // MyError on line 500
```

Region Directives

The last two directives are #region and #endregion. They delimit a section of code that can be expanded or collapsed using the outlining feature of Visual Studio.

```
#region MyRegion
#endregion
```

Just as the conditional directives, regions can be nested any number of levels deep.

```
#region MyRegion
 #region MySubRegion
 #endregion
#endregion
```

CHAPTER 26

Delegates

A *delegate* is a type used to reference a method. This allows methods to be assigned to variables and passed as arguments. The delegate's declaration specifies the method signature to which objects of the delegate type can refer. Delegates are by convention named with each word initially capitalized, followed by Delegate at the end of the name.

```
delegate void MyDelegate(string s);
```

A method that matches the delegate's signature can be assigned to a delegate object of this type.

```
class MyClass
{
  static void Print(string t)
  {
    System.Console.WriteLine(t);
  }

  static void Main()
  {
    MyDelegate d = Print;
  }
}
```

© Mikael Olsson 2018
M. Olsson, *C# 7 Quick Syntax Reference*, https://doi.org/10.1007/978-1-4842-3817-2_26

This delegate object will behave as if it were the method itself, regardless of whether it refers to a static or an instance method. A method call on the object will be forwarded by the delegate to the method, and any return value will be passed back through the delegate.

```
MyDelegate d = Print;
d("Hello"); // "Hello"
```

The syntax used here to instantiate the delegate is actually a simplified notation that was introduced in C# 2.0. The backwards compatible way to instantiate a delegate is to use the regular reference type initialization syntax.

```
MyDelegate d = new MyDelegate(Print);
```

Anonymous Methods

C# 2.0 also introduced anonymous methods, which can be assigned to delegate objects. An anonymous method is specified by using the delegate keyword followed by a method parameter list and body. This can simplify the delegate's instantiation since a separate method will not have to be defined in order to instantiate the delegate.

```
MyDelegate f = delegate(string t)
{
  System.Console.WriteLine(t);
};
```

Lambda Expressions

C# 3.0 went one step further and introduced lambda expressions. They achieve the same goal as anonymous methods, but with a more concise syntax. A lambda expression is written as a parameter list followed by the lambda operator (=>) and an expression.

```
delegate int MyDelegate(int i);

static void Main()
{
  // Anonymous method
  MyDelegate a = delegate(int x) { return x * x; };

  // Lambda expression
  MyDelegate b = (int x) => x * x;

  a(5); // 25
  b(5); // 25
}
```

The lambda must match the signature of the delegate. Typically, the compiler can determine the data type of the parameters from the context, so they do not need to be specified. The parentheses may also be left out if the lambda has only one input parameter.

```
MyDelegate c = x => x * x;
```

If no input parameters are needed, an empty set of parentheses must be specified.

```
delegate void MyEmptyDelegate();
// ...
MyEmptyDelegate d = () => System.Console.WriteLine("Hello");
```

A lambda expression that only executes a single statement is called an *expression lambda*. The expression of a lambda can also be enclosed in curly brackets to allow it to contain multiple statements. This form is called a *statement lambda*.

```
MyDelegate e = (int x) => {
  int y = x * x;
  return y;
};
```

Expression Body Members

Lambda expressions provide a shorthand alternative way to define class members in cases when the member consists of only a single expression. This is called an *expression body definition*. Consider the following class.

```
class Person
{
  public string name { get; } = "John";
  public void PrintName() { System.Console.WriteLine(name); }
}
```

These member bodies can be rewritten as expression bodies instead, which are easier to read.

```
class Person
{
  public string name => "John";
  public void PrintName() => System.Console.WriteLine(name);
}
```

Support for implementing member bodies as lambda expressions was added in C# 6 for methods and get properties. C# 7.0 extended this list of allowed members to also include constructors, destructors, set properties, and indexers. To illustrate, here is an example using expression bodies for a constructor and a property that has both set and get accessors.

```
class Person
{
  private string firstName;
  public string name
  {
    get => firstName;
```

```
  set => firstName = value;
  }
  public Person(string name) => this.name = name;
}
```

Multicast Delegates

It is possible for a delegate object to refer to more than one method. Such an object is known as a multicast delegate and the methods it refers to are contained in a so-called invocation list. To add another method to the delegate's invocation list, either the addition operator or the addition assignment operator can be used.

```
static void Hi()  { System.Console.Write("Hi"); }
static void Bye() { System.Console.Write("Bye"); }
// ...
MyDelegate del = Hi;
del = del + Hi;
del += Bye;
```

Similarly, to remove a method from the invocation list, the subtraction or subtraction assignment operators are used.

```
del -= Hi;
```

When calling a multicast delegate object, all methods in its invocation list will be invoked with the same arguments in the order that they were added to the list.

```
del(); // "HiBye"
```

If the delegate returns a value, only the value of the last invoked method will be returned. Likewise, if the delegate has an out parameter, its final value will be the value assigned by the last method.

Delegate Signature

As mentioned, a method can be assigned to a delegate object if it matches the delegate's signature. However, a method does not have to match the signature exactly. A delegate object can also refer to a method that has a more derived return type than that defined in the delegate, or that has parameter types that are ancestors of the corresponding delegate's parameter types.

```
class Base {}
class Derived : Base {}

delegate Base MyDelegate(Derived d);

class MyClass
{
  static Derived Test(Base o) { return new Derived(); }

  static void Main()
  {
    MyDelegate d = Test;
  }
}
```

Delegates as Parameters

An important property of delegates is that they can be passed as method parameters. To demonstrate the benefit of this, two simple classes will be defined. The first one is a data storage class called PersonDB that has an array containing a couple of names. It also has a method that takes a delegate object as its argument and calls that delegate for each name in the array.

```
delegate void ProcessPersonDelegate(string name);

class PersonDB
{
  string[] list = { "John", "Sam", "Dave" };

  public void Process(ProcessPersonDelegate f)
  {
    foreach(string s in list) f(s);
  }
}
```

The second class is Client, which will use the storage class. It has a Main method that creates an instance of PersonDB, and it calls that object's Process method with a method that is defined in the Client class.

```
class Client
{
  static void Main()
  {
    PersonDB p = new PersonDB();
    p.Process(PrintName);
  }

  static void PrintName(string name)
  {
    System.Console.WriteLine(name);
  }
}
```

The benefit of this approach is that it allows the implementation of the data storage to be separated from the implementation of the data processing. The storage class only handles the storage and has no knowledge of the processing that is done on the data. This allows the storage class to be written in a more general way than if this class had to implement all of the potential processing operations that a client may want to perform on the data. With this solution, the client can simply plug its own processing code into the existing storage class.

CHAPTER 27

Events

Events enable an object to notify other objects when something of interest occurs. The object that raises the event is called the *publisher* and the objects that handle the event are called *subscribers*.

Publisher

To demonstrate the use of events, a publisher will be created first. This will be a class that inherits from `ArrayList`, but this version will raise an event whenever an item is added to the list. Before the event can be created, a delegate is needed that will hold the subscribers. This could be any kind of delegate, but the standard design pattern is to use a `void` delegate that accepts two parameters. The first parameter specifies the source object of the event, and the second parameter is a type that either is or inherits from the `System.EventArgs` class. This parameter usually contains the details of the event, but in this example there is no need to pass any event data and so the base `EventArgs` class will be used as the parameter's type.

```
public delegate void
  EventHandlerDelegate(object sender,
                       System.EventArgs e);

class Publisher : System.Collections.ArrayList
{
  // ...
}
```

© Mikael Olsson 2018
M. Olsson, *C# 7 Quick Syntax Reference*, https://doi.org/10.1007/978-1-4842-3817-2_27

Event Keyword

With the delegate defined, the event can be created in the `Publisher` class using the event keyword followed by the delegate and the name of the event. The event keyword creates a special kind of delegate that can only be invoked from within the class where it is declared. Its access level is public so that other classes are allowed to subscribe to this event. The delegate that follows the event keyword is called the event delegate. The name of the event is commonly a verb. In this case, the event will be raised after the item has been added so the past-tense of the verb "Add" is used, which is "Added". If a pre-event was created instead, which is raised before the actual event, then the gerund (–ing) form of the verb would be used, in this case "Adding".

```
public event EventHandlerDelegate Added;
```

Alternatively, in place of this custom event delegate, the predefined `System.EventHandler` delegate could have been used. This delegate is identical to the one defined previously, and it's used in the .NET class libraries for creating events that have no event data.

Event Caller

To invoke the event, an event caller can be created. The naming convention for this method is to precede the event's name with the word `On`, which in this case becomes `OnAdded`. The method has the protected access level to prevent it from being called from an unrelated class, and it is marked as virtual to allow deriving classes to override it. It takes the event arguments as its one parameter, which in this case is of the `EventArgs` type. The method will raise the event only if it is not null, meaning only when the event has any registered subscribers. To raise the event, the `this` instance reference is passed as the sender, and the `EventArgs` object is the object that was passed to the method.

146

```
protected virtual void OnAdded(System.EventArgs e)
{
  if (Added != null) Added(this, e);
}
```

Raising Events

Now that the class has an event and a method for calling it, the final step is to override the ArrayList's Add method to make it raise the event. In this overridden version of the method the base class's Add method is first called, and the result is stored. The event is then raised with the OnAdded method, by passing to it the Empty field in the System.EventArgs class, which represents an event with no data. Finally, the result is returned to the caller.

```
public override int Add(object value)
{
  int i = base.Add(value);
  OnAdded(System.EventArgs.Empty);
  return i;
}
```

The complete Publisher class now has the following appearance.

```
class Publisher : System.Collections.ArrayList
{
  public delegate void
    EventHandlerDelegate(object sender,
                         System.EventArgs e);

  public event EventHandlerDelegate Added;
```

```
protected virtual void OnAdded(System.EventArgs e)
{
  if (Added != null) Added(this, e);
}

public override int Add(object value)
{
  int i = base.Add(value);
  OnAdded(System.EventArgs.Empty);
  return i;
}
}
```

Subscriber

To use the Publisher class, another class will be created that will subscribe to the event.

```
class Subscriber
{
  //...
}
```

Event Handler

This class contains an event handler, which is a method that has the same signature as the event delegate and is used to handle an event. The name of the handler is commonly the same as the name of the event followed by the EventHandler suffix.

```
class Subscriber
{
  public void AddedEventHandler(object sender,
                                  System.EventArgs e)
  {
    System.Console.WriteLine("AddEvent occurred");
  }
}
```

Subscribing to Events

The Publisher and Subscriber classes are now complete. To demonstrate their use, a Main method is added where objects of the Publisher and Subscriber classes are created. In order to register the handler in the Subscriber object to the event in the Publisher object, the event handler is added to the event as if it were a delegate. Unlike a delegate, however, the event may not be called directly from outside its containing class. Instead, the event can only be raised by the Publisher class, which in this case occurs when an item is added to that object.

```
class MyApp
{
  static void Main()
  {
    Subscriber s = new Subscriber();
    Publisher  p = new Publisher();

    p.Added += s.AddedEventHandler;
    p.Add(10); // "AddEvent occurred"
  }
}
```

CHAPTER 28

Generics

Generics refer to the use of type parameters, which provide a way to design code templates that can operate with different data types. Specifically, it is possible to create generic methods, classes, interfaces, delegates, and events.

Generic Methods

In the following example, there is a method that swaps two integer arguments.

```csharp
static void Swap(ref int a, ref int b)
{
  int temp = a;
  a = b;
  b = temp;
}
```

To make this into a generic method that can work with any data type, a type parameter first needs to be added after the method's name, enclosed between angle brackets. The naming convention for type parameters is that they should start with a capital T, and then have each word that describes the parameter initially capitalized. In cases such as this however, where a descriptive name would not add much value, it is common to simply name the parameter with a capital T.

© Mikael Olsson 2018
M. Olsson, *C# 7 Quick Syntax Reference*, https://doi.org/10.1007/978-1-4842-3817-2_28

```
static void Swap<T>(ref int a, ref int b)
{
  int temp = a;
  a = b;
  b = temp;
}
```

The type parameter can now be used as any other type inside the method, and so the second thing that needs to be done to complete the generic method is to replace the data type that will be made generic with the type parameter.

```
static void Swap<T>(ref T a, ref T b)
{
  T temp = a;
  a = b;
  b = temp;
}
```

Calling Generic Methods

The generic method is now finished. To call it, the desired type argument needs to be specified in angle brackets before the method arguments.

```
int a = 0, b = 1;
Swap<int>(ref a, ref b);
```

In this case, the generic method may also be called as if it were a regular method, without specifying the type argument. This is because the compiler can automatically determine the type since the generic method's parameters use the type parameter. However, if this was not the case, or to use another type argument than the one the compiler would select, the type argument would then need to be explicitly specified.

```
Swap(ref a, ref b);
```

Whenever a generic is called for the first time during runtime, a specialized version of the generic will be instantiated that has every occurrence of the type parameter substituted with the specified type argument. It is this generated method that will be called and not the generic method itself. Calling the generic method again with the same type argument will reuse this instantiated method.

```
Swap<int>(ref a, ref b); // create & call Swap<int>
Swap<int>(ref a, ref b); // call Swap<int>
```

When the generic method is called with a new type, another specialized method will be instantiated.

```
long c = 0, d = 1;
Swap<long>(ref c, ref d); // create & call Swap<long>
```

Generic Type Parameters

A generic can be defined to accept more than one type parameter just by adding more of them between the angle brackets. Generic methods can also be overloaded based on the number of type parameters that they define.

```
static void Dummy<T, U>() {}
static void Dummy<T>() {}
```

Default Value

When using generics, one issue that may arise is how to assign a default value to a type parameter since this value depends on the type. The solution is to use the default keyword followed by the type parameter enclosed in parentheses. This expression will return the default value no matter which type parameter is used.

```
static void Reset<T>(ref T a)
{
  a = default(T);
}
```

Default expressions were enhanced in C# 7.1. As of this version, the type supplied to default may be omitted when the compiler can infer the type based on the context.

```
static void Reset<T>(ref T a)
{
  a = default; // same as default(T)
}
```

Generic Classes

Generic classes allow class members to use type parameters. They are defined in the same way as generic methods, by adding a type parameter after the class name.

```
class Point<T>
{
  public T x, y;
}
```

To instantiate an object from the generic class, the standard notation is used, but with the type argument specified after both class names. Note that in contrast to generic methods, a generic class must always be instantiated with the type argument explicitly specified.

```
Point<short> p = new Point<short>();
```

Generic Class Inheritance

Inheritance works slightly differently with generic classes. A generic class can inherit from a non-generic class, also called a concrete class. Second, it can inherit from another generic class that has its type argument specified, a so-called closed constructed base class. Finally, it can inherit from an open constructed base class, which is a generic class that has its type argument left unspecified.

```
class BaseConcrete  {}
class BaseGeneric<T>{}

class Gen1<T> : BaseConcrete     {} // concrete
class Gen2<T> : BaseGeneric<int>{} // closed constructed
class Gen3<T> : BaseGeneric<T>   {} // open constructed
```

A generic class that inherits from an open constructed base class must define all of the base class's type arguments, even if the derived generic class does not need them. This is because only the child class's type arguments can be sent along when the child class is instantiated.

```
class BaseMultiple<T, U, V> {}
class Gen4<T, U> : BaseMultiple<T, U, int> {}
```

This also means that a non-generic class can only inherit from a closed constructed base class, and not from an open one, because a non-generic class cannot specify any type arguments when it is instantiated.

```
class Con1 : BaseGeneric<int> {} // ok
class Con2 : BaseGeneric<T> {}   // error
```

Generic Interfaces

Interfaces that are declared with type parameters become generic interfaces. Generic interfaces have the same two purposes as regular interfaces. They are either created to expose members of a class that will be used by other classes, or to force a class to implement a specific functionality. When a generic interface is implemented, the type argument must be specified. The generic interface can be implemented by both generic and non-generic classes.

```
// Generic functionality interface
interface IGenericCollection<T>
{
  void store(T t);
}

// Non-generic class implementing generic interface
class Box : IGenericCollection<int>
{
  public int myBox;
  public void store(int i) { myBox = i; }
}

// Generic class implementing generic interface
class GenericBox<T> : IGenericCollection<T>
{
  public T myBox;
  public void store(T t) { myBox = t; }
}
```

Generic Delegates

A delegate can be defined with type parameters. As an example, the following generic delegate uses its type parameter to specify the referable method's parameter. From this delegate type, a delegate object can be created that can refer to any void method that takes a single argument, regardless of its type.

```
class MyClass
{
  public delegate void MyDelegate<T>(T arg);

  public void Print(string s)
  {
    System.Console.Write(s);
  }

  static void Main()
  {
    MyDelegate<string> d = Print;
  }
}
```

Generic Events

Generic delegates can be used to define generic events. For example, instead of using the typical design pattern where the sender of the event is of the Object type, a type parameter can allow the sender's actual type to be specified. This will make the argument strongly-typed, which allows the compiler to enforce that the correct type is used for that argument.

```
delegate void MyDelegate<T, U>(T sender, U eventArgs);
event MyDelegate<MyClass, System.EventArgs> myEvent;
```

Generics and Object

In general, using the Object type as a universal container should be avoided. The reason why Object containers, such as the ArrayList, exist in the .NET class library is because generics were not introduced until C# 2.0. When compared with the Object type, generics not only ensure type safety at compile-time, but they also remove the performance overhead associated with boxing and unboxing value types into an Object container.

```
// Object container class
class MyBox { public object o; }

// Generic container class
class MyBox<T> { public T o; }

class MyClass
{
  static void Main()
  {
    // .NET object container
    System.Collections.ArrayList a;

    // .NET generic container (preferred)
    System.Collections.Generic.List<int> b;
  }
}
```

Constraints

When defining a generic class or method, compile-time enforced restrictions can be applied on the kinds of type arguments that may be used when the class or method is instantiated. These restrictions are called *constraints* and are specified using the where keyword. All in all there are six kinds of constraints.

First, the type parameter can be restricted to value types by using the struct keyword.

```
class C<T> where T : struct {} // value type
```

Second, the parameter can be constrained to reference types by using the class keyword.

```
class D<T> where T : class {}  // reference type
```

Third, the constraint can be a class name. This will restrict the type to either that class or one of its derived classes.

```
class B {}
class E<T> where T : B {}       // be/derive from base class
```

Fourth, the type can be constrained to either be or derive from another type parameter.

```
class F<T, U> where T : U {}   // be/derive from U
```

The fifth constraint is to specify an interface. This will restrict the type parameter to only those types that implement the specified interface, or that is of the interface type itself.

```
interface I {}
class G<T> where T : I {}       // be/implement interface
```

Finally, the type argument can be constrained to only those types that have a public parameterless constructor.

```
class H<T> where T : new() {} // no parameter constructor
```

Multiple Constraints

Multiple constraints can be applied to a type parameter by specifying them in a comma-separated list. Furthermore, to constrain more than one type parameter, additional where clauses can be added. Note that if either the class or the struct constraint is used, it must appear first in the list. Moreover, if the parameterless constructor constraint is used, it must be the last one in the list.

```
class J<T, U>
  where T : class, I
  where U : I, new() {}
```

Why Use Constraints

Aside from restricting the use of a generic method or class to only certain parameter types, another reason for applying constraints is to increase the number of allowed operations and method calls supported by the constraining type. An unconstrained type may only use the System.Object methods. However, by applying a base class constraint, the accessible members of that base class also become available.

```
class Person
{
  public string name;
}
class PersonNameBox<T> where T : Person
{
  public string box;
```

```
  public void StorePersonName(T a)
  {
    box = a.name;
  }
}
```

The following example uses the parameterless constructor constraint. This constraint enables new objects of the type parameter to be instantiated.

```
class MyClass<T> where T : new() {}
```

Note that if a class has a constraint on its type parameter, and a child of that class has a type parameter that's constrained by the base class, that constraint must also be applied to the child class's type parameter.

```
class MyChild<T> : MyClass<T>
  where T : MyClass<T>, new() {}
```

CHAPTER 29

Constants

A variable in C# can be made into a compile-time constant by adding the `const` keyword before the data type. This modifier means that the variable cannot be changed and it must therefore be assigned a value at the same time as it is declared. Any attempts to assign a new value to the constant will result in a compile-time error.

Local Constants

A local constant must always be initialized at the same time as it is declared.

```
static void Main()
{
  const int a = 10; // compile-time constant
}
```

The `const` modifier creates a compile-time constant, and so the compiler will replace all usage of the constant with its value. The assigned value must therefore be known at compile-time. As a result of this, the `const` modifier may only be used together with the simple types, as well as with enum and string types.

© Mikael Olsson 2018
M. Olsson, *C# 7 Quick Syntax Reference*, https://doi.org/10.1007/978-1-4842-3817-2_29

Constant fields

The const modifier can be applied to a field to make the field unchangeable.

```
class MyClass
{
  const int b = 5; // compile-time constant field
}
```

Constant fields cannot have the static modifier. They are implicitly static and are accessed in the same way as static fields.

```
int a = MyClass.b;
```

Readonly

Another variable modifier similar to const is readonly, which creates a runtime constant. This modifier can be applied to fields, and like const, it makes the field unchangeable.

```
class MyClass
{
  readonly int c = 3; // run-time constant field
}
```

Since a readonly field is assigned at runtime, it can be assigned a dynamic value that is not known until runtime.

```
readonly int d = System.DateTime.Now.Hour;
```

Unlike const, readonly can be applied to any data type.

```
readonly int[] e = { 1, 2, 3 }; // readonly array
```

Additionally, a readonly field cannot only be initialized when it is declared. It can also be assigned a value in the constructor.

```
class MyClass
{
  readonly string s;
  public MyClass() { s = "Hello World"; }
}
```

As of C# 7.2, the readonly modifier can be applied to not just fields but also to structs. Declaring a struct as readonly will enforce immutability on the members of the struct, requiring all fields and properties to be made readonly.

```
readonly struct MyStruct
{
  public readonly int myVar;
  public int myProperty { get; }
  public MyStruct(int var, int prop)
  { .
    myVar = var;
    myProperty = prop;
  }
}
```

Another addition in C# 7.2 is the ability to mark a method's return value as readonly when returning a value type by reference with the ref modifier. This will disallow the caller from modifying the returned value, provided that the returned value is also assigned as a readonly reference and not just a copy.

```
class MyClass
{
  readonly static int i;
  static ref readonly int GetValue() { return ref i; }

  static void Main()
  {
    ref readonly int a = ref GetValue();
    a = 5; // error: readonly variable
  }
}
```

In Parameters

Similar to the ref parameter modifier, C# 7.2 added the in modifier, which
provides the ability to pass an argument as a readonly reference. Any code
in the method that attempts to modify an in parameter (or its members in
the case of a struct) will fail at compile-time and so the parameter must
be initialized prior to the method call.

```
class MyApp
{
  static void Test(in int num)
  {
    // num = 5; // error: readonly parameter
  }

  static void Main()
  {
    int i = 10;
    Test(i); // passed by readonly reference
    Test(2); // allowed, temporary variable created
  }
}
```

Like the ref modifier, the in modifier prevents unnecessary copies from being made of value types. This is useful for performance reasons, particularly when passing a large struct object to a method that's called multiple times.

Constant Guideline

In general, it is a good idea to always declare variables as const or readonly if they do not need to be reassigned. This ensures that the variables will not be changed anywhere in the program by mistake, which in turn helps to prevent bugs. It also clearly conveys to other developers when a variable is intended not to be modified.

CHAPTER 30

Asynchronous Methods

An *asynchronous method* is a method that can return before it has finished executing. Any method that performs a potentially long-running task, such as accessing a web resource or reading a file, can be made asynchronous to improve the responsiveness of the program. This is especially important in graphical applications, because any method that takes a long time to execute on the user interface thread will cause the program to be unresponsive while waiting for that method to complete.

The async and await Keywords keez

Introduced in C# 5, the `async` and `await` keywords allow asynchronous methods to be written with a simple structure that is similar to synchronous (regular) methods. The `async` modifier specifies that the method is asynchronous and that it can therefore contain one or more await expressions. An await expression consists of the `await` keyword followed by an awaitable method call.

© Mikael Olsson 2018
M. Olsson, *C# 7 Quick Syntax Reference*, https://doi.org/10.1007/978-1-4842-3817-2_30

```
class MyApp
{
  async void MyAsync()
  {
    System.Console.Write("A");
    await System.Threading.Tasks.Task.Delay(2000);
    System.Console.Write("C");
  }
}
```

This method will run synchronously until the await expression is reached, at which point the method is suspended and execution returns to the caller. The awaited task is scheduled to run in the background on the same thread. In this case the task is a timed delay that will complete after 2000 milliseconds. Once the task is complete the remainder of the async method will execute.

Calling the async method from Main will output "A" followed by "B" and then "C" after the delay. Note the use of the ReadKey method here to prevent the console program from exiting before the async method has finished.

```
static void Main()
{
  new MyApp().MyAsync();
  System.Console.Write("B");
  System.Console.ReadKey();
}
```

Async return types

In C# 5 an async method can have one of three built-in return types: Task<T>, Task, and void. Specifying Task or void denotes that the method does not return a value, whereas Task<T> means it will return a value of type T. In contrast to void, the Task and Task<T> types are awaitable, so a caller can use the await keyword to suspend itself until after the task has finished. The void type is mainly used to define async event handlers, as event handlers require a void return type.

Custom async methods

In order to call a method asynchronously it has to be wrapped in another method that returns a started task. To illustrate, the following method defines, starts and returns a task which takes 2000 milliseconds to execute before it returns the letter "Y". The task is here defined through the use of a lambda expression for conciseness.

```
using System.Threading.Tasks;
using System.Threading;
// ...
Task<string> MyTask()
{
  return Task.Run<string>( () => {
    Thread.Sleep(2000);
    return "Y";
  });
}
```

This task method can be called asynchronously from an async method. The naming convention for these methods is to append "Async" to the method name. The asynchronous method in this example awaits the result of the task and then prints it.

```
async void MyTaskAsync()
{
  string result = await MyTask();
  System.Console.Write(result);
}
```

The async method is called in the same way as a regular method, as can be seen in the following Main method. The output of the program will be "XY".

```
static void Main()
{
  new MyApp().MyTaskAsync();
  System.Console.Write("X");
  System.Console.ReadKey();
}
```

Extended return types

C# 7.0 lessened the restriction on what return types an async method can have. This can be useful when an async method returns a constant result or is likely to complete synchronously, in which case the extra allocation of a Task object may become an undesired performance cost. The condition is that the returned type must implement the GetAwaiter method, which returns an awaiter object. To make use of this new feature .NET provides the ValueTask<T> type, which is a lightweight value type that includes this method.

To give an example, the following PowTwo async method gives the result of the argument raised to the second power (a^2). It executes synchronously if the argument is less than plus or minus ten, and therefore returns a ValueTask<double> type in order to not have to allocate a Task object in such a case. Note that the Main method here has the async modifier. This is allowed as of C# 7.1 and is used for cases like this when the Main method calls an async method directly.

```
using System.Threading.Tasks;
public class MyAsyncValueTask
{
  static async Task Main()
  {
    double d = await PowTwo(10);
    System.Console.WriteLine(d); // "100"
  }

  private static async ValueTask<double> PowTwo(double a)
  {
    if (a < 10 && a > -10) { return System.Math.Pow(a, 2); }
    return await Task.Run(() => System.Math.Pow(a, 2));
  }
}
```

To use the ValueTask type you need to add a NuGet package to your project. NuGet is a package manager providing free and open-source extensions to Visual Studio. The package is added by right-clicking References in the Solution Explorer and choosing Manage NuGet Packages. Switch to the Browse tab and search for "Tasks" to find the System.Threading. Tasks.Extensions package. Select this package and click install.

Index

A

Abstract
  classes and interfaces, 103–104
  GetArea, 102–103
  members, 101–102
Access levels
  guideline, 79
  inner classes, 78
  internal, 75
  private, 73–74
  private protected, 76
  protected, 74
  protected internal, 76
  public, 77
  top-level, 78
Accessors, 87
Arithmetic operators, 15
Arrays
  access, 26
  allocation, 25
  assignment, 26
  declaration, 25
  definition, 25
  jagged, 27
  rectangular, 26
Assignment operators
  combined, 16

increment and decrement
  operators, 16–17
Asynchronous methods
  async and await keywords,
    169–170
  custom, 171–172
  extended return types, 172–173
  return types, 170
Auto-implemented property, 91

B

Base keyword, 69–71
Binary operator overloading, 122
Bitwise operators, 18
Bool type, 13

C

Calling methods, 38
Catch block, 114–115
Char type, 13
Class
  accessing object members, 50
  constructor, 50–51
    chaining, 53
    default, 54
    overloading, 52

© Mikael Olsson 2018
M. Olsson, *C# 7 Quick Syntax Reference*, https://doi.org/10.1007/978-1-4842-3817-2

CPSIA information can be obtained
at www.ICGtesting.com
Printed in the USA
LVHW08s0749201018
594106LV00018B/35/P